Introductio~

Barmouth (Abermaw) and th~ ... with its surrounding hills and mount~· ... reas in Wales. Lying within the Sno~ ... ·y has attracted many famous travel ... ιbing the estuary as 'sublime'. By thι ... ιving port with many shipyards operating a ... ιerging as a hol-iday resort as sea-bathing became ... ιval of the railway in 1867 across the magnificent railwa⟩ ... ιt precipitating the decline in the shipping industry, brought i ... ᵧ more visitors, drawn by sand, sea, the curative powers of scurvy grass, and the mountainous hinterland. Barmouth rapidly developed into an important Victorian sea-side resort.

Across the mouth of the estuary lies Fairbourne with its famous narrow gauge steam railway. Inland, the wooded slopes above the estuary rise north to the foothills of the Rhinogs, and south to the Cadair Idris range. These upland areas are crossed by important ancient trackways and are rich in prehistoric sites and monuments, including hillforts, standing stones and burial chambers. They also contain slate quarries, manganese workings and the famous gold-mines above Bontddu.

The 26 circular walks in this fully revised new edition comprehensively explore the area's coast, estuary, hills, and upland valleys, as well as its fascinating history, using the network of good paths, ancient green upland roads, tramways and the former railway line, now the Mawddach Trail, running along the estuary. They offer superb views and pass many sites of historical interest. Most are accessible by public transport.

The routes, which range from an easy 1¼ mile woodland walk to a exhilarating 10 mile upland circuit, are well within the capability of most people. They follow public rights of way or permissive paths, and cross Open Access land. A key feature is that individual routes, as well as containing shorter walk options, can easily be linked to provide longer and more challenging day walks, if required. Be properly prepared and equipped for any upland walk, where weather conditions can quickly change. Walking boots are required, along with provisions, map and appropriate clothing to protect against the elements. Please remember that path conditions can vary according to season and weather. If you encounter any problems with paths, please refer these to Gwynedd Council Highways Department (01766 771000).

Each walk has a detailed map and description which enables the route to be followed without difficulty, but be aware that changes in detail can occur at any time. The location of each walk is shown on the inside cover and a summary of their key features is also given. This includes an estimated walking time, but allow more time to enjoy the scenery. Please observe the country code and respect any ancient site visited.

Enjoy your walking!

DINAS OLEU & THE PANORAMA WALK

DESCRIPTION This 3¾ mile walk (**A**) features two of Barmouth's natural attractions, popular with visitors since the 19thC – Dinas Oleu, the rugged hillside overlooking the town and the first property given to the National Trust after its foundation in 1895; and the famous Panorama Walk – both offering stunning views of the area. Allow about 2½ hours. A shorter 1¼ mile walk of Dinas Oleu (**B**) is included.
START The Railway Station, Barmouth. [SH 613159]

Dinas Oleu was donated by Mrs Fanny Talbot and aptly fulfills the stated desire of creating 'open-air sitting rooms for city dwellers to have a place to breathe'. She also gave 13 cottages to her close friend, writer, art critic and social reformer John Ruskin to further his experiments in social living. One of his first tenants was Auguste Guyard, known locally as 'The Frenchman' He worked tirelessly, instructing local people on horticultural matters and the virtues of a frugal industrious life, until his death in 1883. He is buried on the hillside. Mothers used to bring children suffering from whooping cough onto Dinas Goleu to benefit from the seaborne air.

I Go along Station Road ahead towards Barmouth's main street. At the junction, turn RIGHT, then go along the first road on the left (Water Street). Shortly, turn LEFT up Tan-y-Graig and follow the oak leaf Dinas Oleu signs, soon going up the lane's right fork. Continue up a path, soon bending sharp LEFT up to reach an information board at a good viewpoint. Go up the path past the nearby metal NT Dinas Oleu sign. At a path junction where the right fork angles up the slope, keep ahead to follow a more gently rising path across the gorse covered slope past a stone seating area, after which it bends sharp RIGHT up the hillside. You pass a side path on the left, then one on your right (which you will soon follow), before bending LEFT to reach a stone semi-circular viewing platform. *Built in 1995 to commemorate the National Trust's centenary, it offers splendid views overlooking Barmouth, the mouth of the Mawddach estuary to Fairbourne and along the coast to Pembrokeshire. Also northwards to Shell Island, and the Lleyn Peninsular extending to Bardsey Island. Near the harbour is the distinctive old Round House, built in 1834.* Return down the path and turn LEFT on the first side path. Follow it across the slope and down to go through a small wooden gate in the wall.

2 Go up the path and past the entrance to the Frenchman's Grave – *which you may wish to visit.* Continue alongside the wall to reach a seat just beyond its corner – *offering views across the Mawddach estuary to the Cadair Idris range.* At a waymarked path junction beyond take the LEFT fork. (For **Walk B** go down its right fork. Just before a small iron gate, turn right to rejoin Walk A, soon on a descent down the '100 steps'.) Follow the path up to a small iron gate, then continue up the path. After about 20 yards it bends LEFT up towards the wall, before moving away to rise steadily across the attractive craggy gorse and heather covered hillside to go through a small iron gate in the wall. The path rises to another gate, then beneath 'The Slabs' – *popular with rock climbers* – to reach a lane.

3 Turn RIGHT and follow the lane down the hillside to a junction with Panorama Road. Turn RIGHT down the road past the Snowdonia National Park Panorama car park, then go through a gate on the left on the signed Panorama Walk. Follow the path up the hillside and into a wood, descending between walls. After a large wooden gate immediately turn RIGHT through an adjoining iron gate – signposted Panorama Walk. *In the early 1880s, a penny was charged by Mr Davies of the Corsygedol Hotel for entry via a 'toll-wicket' here, causing people to grumble*

2

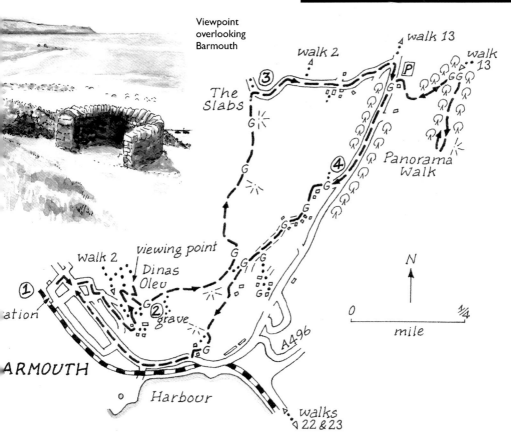

Viewpoint overlooking Barmouth

and write to the papers. A commentator at the time said that without his enterprise the 'View' would have been lost to the public altogether! Follow the path up through the trees. When it splits, take the LEFT fork and follow the path up to the open rocky summit, where a wooden seat makes an excellent stopping place to take in the magnificent views over the tidal Mawddach estuary to the coast. Complete the Panorama circuit then retrace your steps back to the road. Continue down the road, past the entrance to Hafod-y-Bryn.

4 Shortly take a signposted path angling up a track on the right. Just before a gate, turn RIGHT up steps to a small iron gate. Continue alongside the fence to pass behind the house. At its corner, turn LEFT down the walled path to a gate. Continue past a house, and at another bear RIGHT along a walled track to pass between stone buildings. Continue up the track, shortly descending to the gated entrance to Caefadog. Here, turn RIGHT to go through a small iron gate. Turn LEFT (or continue up the path ahead to return along your outward route). Walk alongside the wall to a small iron gate, after which the path descends beside a wall past nearby Caefadog Fach, and continues down to reach a great viewpoint overlooking Barmouth harbour by a disused quarry. Follow the waymarked path to soon descend the stepped path, known locally as the '100 Steps', to the main road. Follow it RIGHT back into the centre of Barmouth.

WALK 2

CERRIG ARTHUR & BWLCH-Y-LLAN

DESCRIPTION A 6 mile walk (**A**) exploring the attractive foothills above Barmouth offering stunning panoramic views. The route climbs up the rugged hillside of Dinas Oleu and on up to 'The Slabs', popular with rock climbers. It then continues up across upland pasture before descending to follow a scenic high-level road to its end and rising to Cerrig Arthur stone circle. The return route is now part of the waymarked Ardudwy Way. It rises steadily on an ancient highway across open slopes to its highest point at 1115 feet/340 metres, then descends Bwlch-y-Llan, before meandering on superb green tracks and paths back to Barmouth, taking in a small side peak on route. Allow about 4 hours. The route also includes shorter described 4¾ mile (**B**) and 2½ mile (**C**) walks.
START The Railway Station, Barmouth [SH 613159]

Cerrig Arthur, set high on the open hillside, is the remains of a Bronze Age circle, possibly a ritual or burial monument. It also lies on the ancient upland route via Bwlch y Llan (the Pass to the Church) followed by inhabitants of Bontddu – a distance of over 5 miles – to worship in the 13thC parish church at Llanaber. Interestingly, the stones stand near the original site planned for Llanaber church, and are known as 'Church Stones'. According to tradition, its foundations were repeatedly demolished at night by an unseen power. The subsequent hearing of a voice crying 'Llanaber, Llanaber' made the terrified men change the location for their parish church.

I Follow the detailed instructions of paragraphs **I** and **2** in **Walk 1A** to reach the lane by 'The Slabs'. (For **Walk C**, turn left, soon passing a ladder-stile on your left, offering an alternative link path, and follow the lane/track to Gellfawr farm. After passing the house, turn left on the signposted path to rejoin the main route at point 5.)

2 For **Walk A/B** turn RIGHT down the lane to a ladder-stile/ gate. A little further take a signposted path through a small gate on the left into Open Access land. Follow the path up the hillside to a superb viewpoint. The path then rises along a small ridge, before levelling out to go through a wall gap. *Ahead is a transmitter mast and the distant Diffwys ridge beyond.* After another wall gap, the path bends LEFT up near the wall. After crossing a ladder-stile in it keep ahead to reach a wall corner beneath buildings and the transmitter mast. (For **Walk B**, turn left alongside the wall, then follow a path up the hillside ahead to a kissing gate in a wall. Rejoin the main route just ahead at point 4)

3 For **Walk A**, cross the ladder-stile and follow the path between walls – *with a good view of the Cadair Idris range ahead –* soon descending then bending LEFT beside a wall. After a wall-gap the path descends between walls to a ladder-stile/gate to join a road below. Follow the road past cottages, later rising. After a gate, the road bends down to nearby Sylfaen farm. Here take the signposted path through double gates ahead and follow a stony track past a large barn and up to a gate. Just beyond, go half-LEFT to follow a green track up to the three remaining stones of Cerrig Arthur circle. Here turn LEFT to go through a large wooden gate to join the waymarked Ardudwy Way. Follow the wall on your left across upland pasture, After passing a ruined barn continue along a faint green track – *the old church route* – to go through a gate in the wall corner by sheepfolds. Continue ahead up the hillside to a ladder-stile/gate. The path continues to rise steadily before levelling out at a wall corner to reach another ladder-stile/gate ahead. The path now goes along a small ridge, being joined by Walk B from a nearby kissing gate.

4 The path soon bears RIGHT to join the wall and steadily descends Bwlch-y-Llan. Later turn sharp LEFT down a path to a ladder-stile/ gate in the wall. Continue on a delightful narrow green track – *with views* across to Shell Island and the Lleyn peninsula beyond – later descending to a ladder-stile/gate. Follow the green track down to Gellfawr farm. Pass between outbuildings, then just before the house, turn RIGHT on a signposted path along a green track.

5 Go past a ruin, and at a waymarked fence corner, turn LEFT alongside the fence to reach a small iron gate and a tiny stone slab footbridge over a stream. Angle RIGHT through a reedy area and on through a nearby gateway in the wall. Follow a green track above a small wooded dingle. Just before a gap in a low wall, turn LEFT and follow the

Cerrig Arthur

barn on the seaward side, turn RIGHT to follow a path across the field, through another wall gap and on to a small iron gate ahead giving access to a cairn on the top of Craig-y-Gigfran (Ravens Rock). *Known locally as 'The Peak', it offers superb coastal views. On the cairn is a plaque erected to the memory of soldiers from Birmingham killed in 1916.* Return to the barn.

6 Continue down the walled green track and through a gate. Follow this superb green track down the hillside overlooking Barmouth, passing old manganese mine workings and a ruin. Soon it bends down RIGHT. (To maintain height a little longer here go up another green track, through a gate. Shortly go through a small gate below to reach the viewing platform again. Follow a path right, soon descending via a zig-zag to rejoin the main route by a metal fence. Follow it left to the lane.) For the main route continue down the track, soon bending LEFT. When it does a sharp U-turn right to gates go down a path ahead to a small wooden gate, and on down to a lane. Turn RIGHT down the lane to join your outward route.

wall down to the ruins of Cellfechan farm. *In the 1920s the farm was owned by the Urban District Council and provided refreshments to passing walkers.* Just before the large stone

WALK 3

BWYLCH Y RHIWGYR

DESCRIPTION A 7¼ mile (**A**) or 6½ mile (**B**) walk for experienced walkers exploring foothills and high mountain passes north of Barmouth following ancient trackways, old bridleways, miners paths and tramways. It features extensive remnants of 19thC manganese mining. The route rises past an ancient hillfort to the top of Bwylch y Llan (1115 feet)/340 metres on part of an ancient route between Bontddu and 13thC St Mary's church at Llanaber. It then continues to Bwylch y Rhiwgyr (1509 feet/460 metres) either by an undulating ridge reaching a height of 1696 feet/ 517 metres (Walk A) or by the Ardudwy Way and Cerrig Arthur stone circle (Walk B). After descending the narrow pass, used by drovers and travellers for centuries, the route passes old manganese mine workings, before descending to St Mary's church (Walk A) or on a more direct route (Walk B). Allow about 4½ hours.

START Lay-by, Llanaber [SH 605173]

DIRECTIONS Leave Barmouth on the A496 towards Harlech. Shortly after entering Llanaber, there is a lay-by on the left by a telephone box. Park tidily on the right side. The walk is also accessible by bus and train.

I Cross the road and go up the nearby access lane to Ceilwart Uchaf. Shortly, take a signposted path through a small gate on the left. Follow the path alongside a stream, and on through a small waymarked gate above a garage. Follow the wall on your right up through a gateway, over a stream and up to a ladder-stile. Go up the waymarked path through gorse and bracken and on alongside a wall to a ladder-stile/gate. Continue between walls and briefly alongside the wall on your left, then go along a short grassy shelf to cross a ladder-stile. Turn RIGHT and follow a walled path up the hillside to a green track. Turn RIGHT up the walled track – *the church route* – to a gate into Open Access land.

2 Cross a nearby ladder-stile, and follow the old green trackway up the rocky hillside. After a gate bear LEFT up the main track, which rises steadily past a Romano British hillfort, then an old incline, to a ladder-stile/gate to re-enter Open Access. *Ore from the Hafotty manganese mine was brought down this gravity incline and continued on a tramway for a final descent by ropeway.* Follow the track across the hillside, shortly joining the waymarked Ardudwy Way on a climb up Bwylch y Llan. At the top of the pass follow the path round and across a small ridge to cross a ladder-stile by a gate.

3 For **Walk A** turn LEFT to follow the wall up onto the ridge. Go past a ladder-stile, then continue on a good stiled path by the wall along the undulating ridge past a trig point, Bwlch Cwmmaria, then a stone cairn at the highest point, before descending to Bwylch y Rhiwgyr (point 4). For **Walk B** continue ahead with the Ardudwy Way, soon descending to a ladder-stile, then a gate by sheepfolds. Keep ahead, past a ruined stone barn and on to a gate in the wall corner to reach the remains of Carreg Arthur stone circle beyond (see **Walk 2**). Now turn LEFT up to go through a gate. Continue up a green track to join a wall on your left. Shortly, go through a gate in the wall. Turn RIGHT and follow a path just above the wall. Later angle slightly away to a stile in an old gateway. Go through wall gap ahead, then angle LEFT up the tussocky slope to a gate. Follow the green track up to Bwylch y Rhiwgyr.

4 Go through the iron gate and follow the old stony route down the narrow pass to a gate. Here you leave the Ardudwy Way. Turn LEFT on a signposted path and follow the wall across tussocky terrain to go through a gap in the wall corner. Keep ahead on the higher of two paths, soon being joined by another. Follow the path across the

6

pass a small ruin to cross a ladder-stile. *The area ahead contains deep underground and large opencast workings of the Hafotty mine (1885-94). It was the largest manganese mine in Merioneth, employing at its peak 37 men underground and 15 on the surface, producing 12,000 tons of ore for Mostyn Ironworks in Flintshire.* Continue up the hillside to cross a ladder-stile.

5 Cross a narrow grass-topped stone bridge over the workings. After a few yards follow the path ahead to descend the stony hillside to cross a ladder-stile. The path now meanders through gorse and stone, before descending through gorse to a ladder-stile on your left. Continue ahead down a wide path past a ruin. When it fades keep ahead across a reedy area towards a wall, then bear RIGHT across drier ground to a small cairn to follow a path through gorse to cross a ladder-stile in the wall. Turn RIGHT to follow a path leading away from the wall to join a wider path which descends the gorse covered hillside. As it nears a wall it bends down right. Follow a choice of paths down through gorse to a small gate in the corner. Keep ahead, soon joining your outward route. Go along the walled track then follow the green track down upland pasture.

6 Just before a ladder stile/ gate, you have a choice. (For **Walk B** turn LEFT and descend the hillside to join a green track angling down to a familiar ladder-stile. Go through a small gate just below. Follow the path down through bracken, soon bending right down to a waymarked small gate. Descend the narrow walled path, then track to reach the A496. Turn LEFT.) For **Walk A** cross the ladder-stile and descend the track. When it bends left, follow the waymarked path ahead to a ladder-stile. Keep ahead, then bend LEFT to go down a delightful walled bridleway. At the bottom bend RIGHT, then turn LEFT through a gate and descend a lane to cross the A496. Turn LEFT. After visiting the church continue along the road.

slope, soon taking its right fork to gradually descend to a wall corner by old workings. Follow the path leading away from the wall corner past more workings then follow the wall on your right to a hidden ladder-stile into Open Access land. *The Egryn manganese mine worked this area, mainly underground by levels and shafts in two periods: 1835-40 and 1917-24. From its northern end a 1¼ mile aerial ropeway took ore down to Egryn Abbey.* Continue ahead over two further ladder-stiles to reach the top of the rise ahead. Follow a path LEFT up near the wall. Shortly, angle RIGHT up the slope to join a level narrow green track – *a former 2 ft gauge tramway.* Follow it past old workings and on down to a ladder-stile. Continue with the old tramway, soon descending to

MYNYDD EGRYN

DESCRIPTION A 4 mile walk on the foothills and upland shelf adjoining the coast between Llanaber and Tal-y-bont, featuring ancient sites and monuments of significant archaeological interest. The route passes the old house of Egryn Abbey, now owned by the National Trust, then rises steadily up to cross the expansive wild treeless exposed Mynydd Egryn, featuring the impressive Carneddau Hengwn burial chambers of multi-period construction, dating from the 3rd millennium, then a Bronze Age ring cairn at a height of just over 1000 feet. The route then returns via the Iron Age fort of Pen y Dinas. Allow about 3 hours.

START Capel Egryn [SH 594205]

DIRECTIONS One mile south of Tal-y-bont on the A496 by an old chapel. The start is on a bus route – the stop is called 'Sunday School'.

I Cross the road and walk along the pavement towards Barmouth. Shortly, take a signposted path along a track on the left leading to Egryn. Follow the track past the complex of buildings at Egryn dating from the 16thC, and now a working farm. *This site is reputed to have been an earlier grange of the Cistercian Cymmer Abbey and once a hospital for the poor and wayfarers.* At a track junction keep ahead to go through a waymarked gate. Follow the track over the nearby Ceunant Egryn and on through another gate. Continue along the rougher green track past a stone barn, and on alongside the river. Shortly, take the right fork up the hillside, past a telegraph pole. As the track bends right at the fence corner, keep ahead to cross a waymarked stile in the wall above. Go up the slope to join a green track above. The track soon bends right and rises up the hillside, briefly running alongside a wall, before suddenly levelling out to give extensive all round views. *Ahead over the expanse of Mynydd Egryn is the long bare ridge leading up to Diffwys, and further north the rounded hill of Moelfre. There are views along the coast to Shell Island, the Lleyn peninsula, Bardsey Island, and to the central mountains of Snowdonia. The slopes of the nearby Ceunant Egryn valley were worked for slate in the 1890s, employing nine men, and later for manganese.* Continue ahead on the faint green track.

2 Shortly bear LEFT over a drainage gully and continue along a path. *Ahead on the skyline is the distinctive shape of Pen y Dinas prehistoric hillfort.* Soon bend RIGHT to go through a waymarked gate. Continue ahead across the expansive reedy tussocky terrain, wet in places, towards a distant metal inverted V pole. *Built of bullhead rails, this is the only remaining pylon – the rest were wooden – of the 1½ mile aerial ropeway that carried ore down from the Egryn manganese mine to Egryn Abbey, from where it was taken by cart to Tal-y-bont.* Eventually you reach the corner of the wall on your left. Turn LEFT alongside the wall to see the Carneddau Hengwn burial chambers. Afterwards either return to the wall corner and follow a clear path up to a Bronze Age ring cairn, or angle up the hillside directly to it. *The cairn, with its distinctive outward leaning stones, was used for burial and ceremonial purposes. Just to its east are the remains of a settlement enclosure.* Continue towards a ladder-stile by a gateway ahead, then follow the wall LEFT to cross another ladder-stile in the corner. Keep ahead then turn LEFT away from another nearby ladder-stile, soon descending a small stone covered slope.

3 Head half-RIGHT down the tussocky field to go through a gate in the wall by a small wet reedy area, and across the infant Ceunant Egryn. Angle LEFT to join a faint track which passes through a gap in the wall ahead. Follow the green track – *with Carneddau Hengwn burial chambers visible on the other side of the valley* – across the reedy upland pasture, later moving nearer the wall on your right to cross a stream. Continue near the wall to go through a gate in the corner. Go past stone sheepfolds on your left, then follow a faint narrow green track through a wall gap ahead and on past the southern slopes of Pen y Dinas hillfort to reach a prominent viewpoint. The track

Carneddau Hengwn

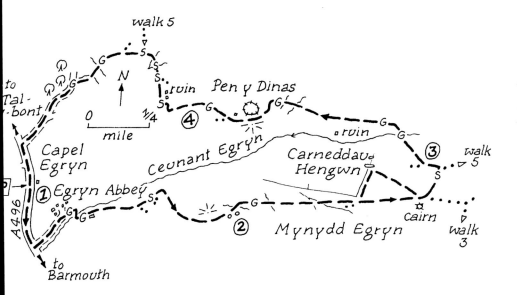

now begins to descend. After passing a small stone ruin on your right, when the path bears half-left, keep straight ahead down the hillside to a small gate in a wall. Descend to a wall corner below.

4 Continue down the hillside, moving slightly closer towards a ruined farmstead to reach a gap in an old wall, in line with the ruin. Turn RIGHT to cross a nearby ladder-stile. Go past the delightful ruin, and through an open gateway directly ahead, and on to cross a ladder-stile. Go along a track and over another ladder-stile by a stream. After another stream the track descends. Very soon cross a ladder-stile on the left and follow the old walled bridleway down the hillside, then the wall on your left to a gate. Continue down to go through an old gateway in the wall ahead. Keep ahead down the next field to follow a faint green track, soon passing through bracken then an iron gate onto a track. Follow it LEFT, and at a track junction bear RIGHT. Follow the track to the A496 and on along the pavement back to the start.

9

WALK 5
PEN Y DINAS

DESCRIPTION A 6 mile walk in the foothills adjoining the coast near Tal-y-bont, featuring several ancient sites of archaeological interest, and good views. The route heads inland up to the prehistoric hillfort of Pen y Dinas situated at over 750 feet. It then crosses a large expanse of more exposed upland pasture to visit a Bronze Age burial and settlement site, rising easily to a height of over 1200 feet to reach the ancient mountain trackway below Bwlch y Rhiwgyr. It returns by paths, tracks and lane past other ancient sites for a finish at a riverside inn. Allow about 4 hours.

START Tal-y-bont [SH 589218]

DIRECTIONS Tal-y-bont lies on the A496 north of Barmouth. The small car park with toilets adjoins the bridge over the river.

I Cross the nearby footbridge over the Afon Ysgethin and walk along the pavement by the A496. Shortly, turn LEFT along Ffordd Tyddyn Felin. Follow this country road for nearly half a mile, later rising past the entrance to Ty'n y Felin and a signposted path on the left. On the next bend, go through a large gate ahead, by a sign 'Hwylfa Porth Egryn'. Now follow a green track rising steadily up the hillside, through a gate and on up to another gate into a walled track. Turn RIGHT and follow the delightful green track across the hillside – *enjoying extensive coastal views* – crossing two ladder-stiles. As the track bends left up towards farm buildings, keep ahead to go through a waymarked gateway. Continue past the ivy covered ruined upland farmstead and over a ladder-stile. Bear LEFT a few yards, then RIGHT alongside the old wall.

2 After 10 yards, turn LEFT and work your way up the part bracken covered hillside, aiming for a wall corner on the skyline, to reach a small gate above. Continue ahead, angling away from the wall, to follow a faint path up the thistle/bracken covered slope – *with the distinctive shape of Pen y Dinas ahead* – to join a faint narrow green track which rises just to the right of a small

low stone ruin, then passes over the right shoulder of the hill – *with views ahead over Cwm Egryn to the long ridge leading up to Diffwys* – and on past the southern slopes of Pen y Dinas. *Strategically placed, this prehistoric hillfort has ramparts of earth and stone, with an entrance on its west side.* Follow the track, parallel with a wall on your left, to go through a gap in the wall ahead, and on past stone sheepfolds to go through a gate. Follow the wall on your left through the reedy upland pasture. After about 100 yards, after crossing a stream, follow an old green track a little distance from the wall. Later it moves back towards the wall to go through a gap in the wall ahead. *On route, on the other side of the valley can be seen Carneddau Hengwn prehistoric burial chambers*

3 Keep ahead with the track, then after 30 yards angle RIGHT to go through a gate in the wall by the infant Ceunant Egryn. Head half-LEFT up the tussocky, later stone covered upland pasture to reach two ladder-stiles in the top corner. Cross the one actually in the corner into the adjoining field and continue to a Bronze Age ring cairn with its distinctive outward leaning stones, a little way from the wall. *It was used for burial and ceremonial purposes. Just to its east are the remains of a settlement enclosure.* Return to the ladder-stile, then cross the one ahead and go through a small adjoining gate. Go half-RIGHT, soon joining a path. Go up its RIGHT fork to cross an area of old manganese workings,then the stone covered hillside. Later head up to a small gate near the wall corner into Open Access land. Continue ahead to join the wide path rising up Bwlch y Rhiwgyr. *This is an ancient mountain*

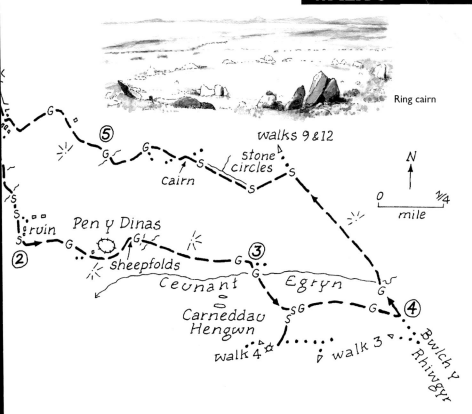

Ring cairn

route connecting Harlech and the coast with Dolgellau (See **Walk 11** for details)

4 Turn LEFT and follow the path down to a gate. Continue with the path alongside the wall and later a fence, where it becomes more a narrow green track. At the end of the fence, cross a stile in it into a field, then follow the wall on your right. *The adjoining field contains the remains of two prehistoric religious and funerary stone circles. The second half of the field is reedy, tussocky and wet in places.* After crossing a ladder-stile in the corner, follow the left bank of a stream to cross a ladder-stile and sleeper bridge. Continue ahead to join a green track by the low mound of an old burial cairn. About 30 yards further, take a path angling RIGHT off the track, soon descending through bracken and gorse to a sleeper bridge and on to go through a facing gate in the field corner.

Angle LEFT then follow a faint green track down the ridged grassy field. At the bottom, bear RIGHT along the track to go through a gate.

5 Follow the track down through three wall gaps and on past a stone ruin to a gate, after which it descends to Eithin Fynydd farm. Turn RIGHT along its access track and continue down the road. *Later, in trees to your left, is the wall-topped circular embankment of an ancient farmstead.* Continue down the road, soon on your outward route. Later take a signposted path through a small gate on the right, and follow the enclosed path through trees to cross a footbridge over the river. Turn LEFT and follow the path alongside the river past another footbridge to reach the Ysgethin Inn – *a former late 19thC woollen mill* – and on back to the start.

WALK 6

MORFA DYFFRYN

DESCRIPTION An easy 3 mile walk featuring open countryside, woodland, an inn midway and the high dunes of Morfa Dyffryn National Nature Reserve and adjoining sandy Benar beach to finish. Allow about 2 hours.
START Snowdonia National Park Traeth Benar car park [SH 573227]
DIRECTIONS Just north of Tal-y-bont take a minor road on the left by a church signposted to Benar Beach/Dyffryn Seaside Estate to find the car park at its end.

1 Return along the road, then after ½ mile go through a kissing gate on the left opposite Ty Bennar. Follow the path through a field, then a wood, over the railway line – heed the signs – and on through further woodland. Turn LEFT along the access track just ahead, then cross a stile on the right. Follow the boundary on the left to a road.

2 Follow it LEFT. At the junction turn LEFT and follow the road past houses, across the gated level crossing at Dyffryn Ardudwy station and past Cadwgan Hotel/Inn. Soon it becomes a stony track which you follow to its end to enter Dyffryn Seaside Estate. Go along the road to a mini roundabout. Follow the road ahead (a bridleway) past the store and country inn, later becoming a stony track, then follow the boardwalked path through the high dunes. Turn LEFT along the beach then leave it at a tall red and white post. Follow a boardwalked path back through the dunes, then the road to the start.

WALK 7

DYFFRYN BURIAL CHAMBERS

DESCRIPTION An easy 3 mile walk featuring impressive ancient burial chambers and an inland section of the Coast Path. Allow about 2 hours..
START Car park, Tal-y-bont [SH 589218]
DIRECTIONS Tal-y-bont lies on on the A496 north of Barmouth. The small car park with toilets adjoins the bridge over the river.

*A*t *Dyffryn Ardudwy is an impressive rectangular Neolithic burial site dating from 4th/early 3rd millennium. It contains two classic chamber tombs of the type (portal dolmens) most commonly found in this area, and on the east coast of Ireland, indicating a movement of early man across the Irish sea. Among the earliest tombs built in Britain, the lower one is the older, whilst the other has produced evidence of a late Bronze Age cremation. As man turned his activities from hunting to farming, and cleared woodland for pasture, settlements were established, and such tombs used for family burials over centuries became a focus for the local community, similar to the later role of churches. They feature tall entrance stones and a small rectangular chamber, generally covered by a large capstone, and are fine examples of early engineering. Such tombs were originally covered by a mound of stones or earth, but as a result of robbers, the chambers have been left exposed.*

1 Head north through the village past the shop, then at the 40 mph road sign, turn RIGHT on a signposted bridleway up a tree-lined lane leading to Bellaport Caravan site. Just beyond the last bungalow, cross a stone stile on your left, then angle RIGHT to a small gate in the facing wall into a field – *with good views to Shell Island and the Lleyn Peninsula.* Keep ahead to a gated stile, then follow the wall on your right to a gate. Angle RIGHT up to join the access track of a nearby house. Follow it past farm buildings to a road and go through the gate opposite. Bear RIGHT up the field to a waymarker post/telegraph pole by the top wall. Continue beside the wall to cross a stone stile. Follow the path through the wood to a gate. At a wall corner just beyond angle LEFT across open ground to pass through bracken to reach a small iron gate by the burial chambers. Follow the path alongside the wall past a gate giving access to the site and down to

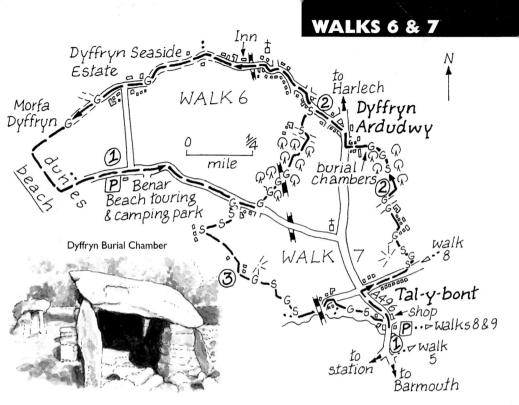

Dyffryn Burial Chamber

the A496 at Dyffryn Ardudwy. Turn RIGHT along the road, then take the first road on the left.

2 Shortly after leaving the village take a signposted path over a stile on the left by a stone barn. Follow the boundary on your right round to another stile. Turn LEFT along an access track, then take a signposted path on the right through a wood. After crossing the railway line – heed the warning signs – continue through further woodland, then across a field to a road by Ty Bennar. Turn RIGHT then take the signposted Coast Path through a small gate by the entrance to Bennar Fawr. Go up the field to a stile. Keep ahead beside the wall on your left, then at a telegraph pole turn RIGHT across the field to a stone stile by a larger telegraph pole. Walk through the next field towards a house to another stone stile in the corner. Turn LEFT along the edge of the next long field, then follow the wide raised path half-RIGHT past a stone barn. Continue to other farm buildings ahead. Turn RIGHT.

3 At the wall corner, turn LEFT and follow the wall round to go through a gate by the waymarked wall end. *To the east is Moelfre and ahead the long ridge leading up to Diffwys.* Bear RIGHT along the field, moving away from the wall to cross a stile in the wall ahead. Angle RIGHT to a way-marked wall corner ahead, then bear LEFT to go through a waymarked gate. Turn right along the field edge to a stone stile in the corner. Just beyond turn LEFT along a track, soon near the river, to pass under the railway line. Turn LEFT along the lane, passing between farm buildings to reach Pandy caravan park. Turn RIGHT through its entrance past reception and static caravans. Keep with the access road's left fork to a gate into a field used for tourers and tents. Go up the field to a small waymarked gate near its right hand corner by the river into Old Mill Park. Go past the end of wooden chalets, then the former corn mill with its waterwheel, and up the access track to the road opposite the shop at Tal-y-bont.

WALK 8

COED CORS-Y-GEDOL

DESCRIPTION A delightful 4¼ mile walk (**A**) or 3 mile walk (**B**) through broadleaf woodland and open country, passing Cors-y-Gedol, one of the area's most historic houses. The route takes you up through the wooded Afon Ysgethin valley to an old drovers halt, then passes a Neolithic burial chamber to reach Cors-y-Gedol. The main route explores the surrounding attractive countryside, before passing through further woodland on its return. Allow about 2½ hours. The route also includes an alternative 2½ mile woodland circuit (**C**).

START Car park, Tal-y-bont [SH 589218]

DIRECTIONS Tal-y-bont lies on on the A496 north of Barmouth. The small car park with toilets adjoins the bridge over the river.

For centuries Cors y Gedol was home to the Vaughans, one of the principal families of Ardudwy. They were descendants of Osborn Fitzgerald (Wyddel), an Irish nobleman, who came to Wales in the 13thC, and who acquired the estate through marriage. Centuries ago most of the surrounding land was marshy, which could help to explain its name meaning 'The bog of hospitality'. For many years they played a prominent role in Meirioneth affairs, serving as MPs, High Sheriffs and Magistrates. In 1791 the family died out and the estate passed to the Mostyns, another aristocratic family, who lived here until 1860. The current mansion, dating from 1576, has undergone considerable alteration and extension, with additional houses and agricultural buildings, reflecting the acquired wealth of successive generations. It lies at the end of a straight drive connecting it with the Vaughan family chapel in Llanddwywe church.

I From the end of the car park, turn LEFT on a path beside the wooded Afon Ysgethin, soon passing the Ysgethin Inn – *a former late 19thC woollen mill, whose porch was built with stone taken from an old drover's inn, Rhos-caerau, on the upland route to*

Bontddu. Go round the right hand end of a small stone building just beyond to rejoin the river. Follow the path past two footbridges and on through the attractive woodland to a ladder-stile/gate. Continue up the wooded valley, later rising away from the river to reach a path junction by a seat. Keep ahead on the wide level path, past a path angling back on the left, after which you again continue close by the river, soon rising to another path junction. (For **Walk C** turn left up the path and follow it back along the top edge of the wood. Shortly, take its left fork on a gentle descent. At a distinct cross-path, turn right and follow a narrow path through the trees, over a faint cross path. At another path junction keep ahead to rejoin the main route just before a stream and a gate. Here turn left along a wide stony path and resume text at the 2nd sentence in paragraph **4**) For the main route, continue ahead above the river, through a small gate, and on up to reach a lane by Lleti Lloegr (The English Shelter). *It was once an an emergency shoeing station and overnight stopping place for 17th/18thC drovers heading for the mountain pass of Bwlch y Rhiwgyr on route to Bontddu. Cattle were kept in five adjoining small fields.*

2 Turn LEFT along the lane, past a Neolithic burial chamber dating from 4th/3rd millennium BC., and on through a gate to a road. *Here are extensive views of the vast upland landscape, with the rounded hilltop of Moelfre, and, further inland, the long ridge leading to Diffwys.* Turn LEFT down the road to the first bend by an entrance to Cors y Gedol. Here you have a choice. (For **Walk B**, continue on the road past numerous stone buildings, then Llys Faen. About 120 yards after bending past the ornate gated entrance to Cors y Gedol Hall take a signposted path through a gate on the left into the wood to rejoin Walk A at point **4**.) For **Walk A**, follow a signposted path along the track ahead, bending past a house then a side track to go through a facing gate ahead. Continue between a wall and a line of mature trees to a gate, and on along the next field edge to a gated stone stile in the corner at a good viewpoint. Angle RIGHT to cross a stream. After a few yards bear LEFT and fol-

Burial Chamber

low a path – *with good views of Shell Island, the Lleyn Peninsula and Bardsey Island* – to go through a gate. Bear LEFT with the path near the wall.

3 At the wall corner, bear RIGHT and follow the path alongside another old wall, soon bending left. Keep ahead along the wide path to join a lane. Follow it LEFT to pass Meifod Isa farm. About 120 yards further take a signposted bridleway through a gate on the left. Follow the boundary on your left round past a metal gate to go through a wooden gate at the end of a stone wall. Follow the bridleway, later through woodland, to a stile. Continue straight ahead across the field to a

gate onto a road by Parc Uchaf. Turn LEFT along the leafy road. Shortly, take a signposted path through a gate on the right into the wood.

4 Go along the path, then after a gate, take the second wider stony path on the right alongside the stream. Follow this path through the wood. At a crossroad of paths near the wood edge, take the right fork ahead to cross a footbridge over the stream, and on through a small gate by Bellaport caravan site. Go down an attractive straight walled lane – *enjoying your last views along the coast and across Cardigan Bay* – to reach the A496. Turn LEFT and walk along the pavement the short distance back to the start.

WALK 9
PONT SCETHIN

DESCRIPTION A 7 mile upland walk featuring the ancient stone bridge of Pont Scethin set in splendid isolation at 1036 feet beneath the foothills of the Rhinogs – an important crossing point for the former Harlech-Dolgellau-London road. The walk follows the Afon Ysgethin through attractive woodland, then an old drovers route across the wild expansive upland valley of Cwm Ysgethin, visiting hidden Llyn Erddyn (optional). It then joins the ancient road to cross Pont Scethin, before returning by an upland bridleway, later passing historic Cors Y Gedol for a woodland finish. Allow about 4 hours.
START Car park, Tal-y-bont [SH 589218] See **Walk 8**.

From the end of the car park, turn LEFT on a path beside the wooded Afon Ysgethin, soon passing the Ysgethin Inn – *a former late 19thC woollen mill*. The next section follows the Ardudwy Way Follow the path past footbridges through the attractive woodland to a ladder-stile/gate, then continue up the wooded valley past side paths to eventually reach a lane by Lleti Lloegr (The English Shelter). Turn RIGHT and follow the lane down over Pont Fadog – *a stone inscription dates it 1762 and names H. Ed(ward) as the mason employed by William Vaughan of Cors y Gedol* – and continue up the lane to go through a gate at its end. Note nearby Scots pines – *a traditional means of guiding drovers to Lleti Loegr.* Continue up to a nearby track junction. Here turn LEFT. The next section follows the Ardudwy Way.

2 Follow the track up to a gate, then up to another into Open Access land. The track continues to rise steadily, passing through two further gates – *with extensive views looking back*. The track continues along the expansive valley to another gate. *Just to the north is the rocky Craig y Dinas, on which is a prehistoric hillfort and settlement.* Continue with the track to skirt the north western side of Llyn Erddyn still hidden by a small rise. *In the mid 19thC the trout caught here before sunrise were considered*

to be the best in the area. It is known as the 'priest lake' from its association with Druids, who reputedly used the large stones along its banks as seats for worshipping, and kept a store of fish at its outlet. After another gate you have a choice. Either continue along the old track – *after a while looking back to see Llyn Erddyn.* Alternatively, to visit Llyn Erddyn itself follow the wall RIGHT across reedy ground to reach the lake, then go along its edge to a nearby wall. Follow the path near the wall, later passing a ladder-

stile in it. *Up to your right is Llawlech.* At the wall corner turn LEFT to rejoin the green track at a gate. Keep ahead along the left fork, over a stream and on through the wide reedy valley – *with your first sight of Pont Scethin.* Eventually you reach a broad cross path at a small stone marker. *This is the old London to Harlech road.*

3 Follow the old road LEFT down to Pont Scethin – *an important crossing point of the Afon Ysgethin on this ancient road used for centuries by travellers and later drovers. It is a delightful place to stop to enjoy the solitude of this remote stone bridge and dippers in the river.* Continue on the line of the old road rising steadily up the hillside. *When it levels out, look for two small prehistoric standing stones on your left.* At a wide track beneath the southern slopes of Moelfre which services Llyn Bodlyn reservoir further up the valley, turn LEFT. Now simply follow the gated track on a long steady descent, later becoming enclosed by walls – *enjoying extensive views.* Just before it bends down to the first gate the Ardudwy Way branches off along the continuing course of the old road.

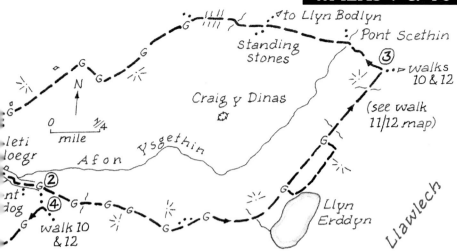

4 Eventually the track becomes a road and passes numerous buildings of historic Cors y Gedol Hall (*See Walk 8*) then Llys Faen. About 120 yards after passing Cors y Gedol's ornate stone gateway, take a signposted path through a gate on the left into the wood. Follow the path to go through a gate, then take the second wider stony path on the right alongside the stream. Follow this path through the wood. At an elongated crossroad of paths near the wood edge, take the LEFT fork, soon bending left. Keep with the wider right fork, go past a descending path on your right to join your outward route just before a seat. Follow it back to the start.

WALK 10
LLAWLECH 1

DESCRIPTION This walk follows the outward route of Walk 9 to join the ancient Harlech-London road rising past the Janet Haigh memorial. It then leads along the 1¾ mile Llawlech ridge and down to Bwlch y Rhiwgyr, before returning down another ancient route, paths and lane. Allow about 6 hours. See **Walk 11** for information on the ancient highways and use the Walk 11/12 map when appropriate. The route is easy to follow but should be avoided in poor visibility.
START As **Walk 9**.

1 & 2 Follow instructions in paragraphs **1-2** of **Walk 9**.

3 Turn RIGHT. (For next section refer to the map on pages 18/19).Follow the old green road up past the memorial to the top of the bwlch by a stone cairn, gate and ladderstile. Turn RIGHT and follow the stiled path alongside the wall on your left across the broad ridge of Llawlech up to the summit cairn and on down to Bwlch y Rhiwgyr. Turn RIGHT down the narrow pass and follow this old route, at first a stony path, then a green track for nearly 2 miles passing through two gates and crossing two ladder-stiles.

4 At a waymark post by a wall on your left, about 100 yards above point **2** of your outward route (map above), turn LEFT. Now follow an old green track near the wall and across the hillside to a gate, and on down towards a house. At a gate by a large stone barn turn LEFT past its stepped end, and follow the path up to a stone stile. Bear RIGHT along the field edge passing above the wall. When it bends right keep ahead to pass through a wall gap, and on to cross a stile in a fence. Go towards a large building ahead and through a small gate in the wall. Follow the walled track RIGHT down to a road. Continue down the road. After about ½ mile, take a signposted enclosed path on the right. Follow it to cross a footbridge over the river to join your outward route.

17

WALK 11

LLAWLECH 2

DESCRIPTION A 6½ mile (**A**) or 5½ mile (**B**) walk for experienced walkers exploring a delightful upland area utilising two old green mountain roads to Harlech and enjoying panoramic views. Walk A climbs to Bwlch y Rhiwgyr (1494 feet), then continues up the Llawlech ridge (1932 feet). Walk B crosses the eastern slopes of Llawlech to join Walk A at another high pass for a splendid return down Braith ridge on another branch of the former Harlech road. Allow about 4 hours. An alternative higher start at the road end shortens the walks by 1⅓ mile.
START Pont Hirgwm [SH 668198] or road end [SH 657202]
DIRECTIONS From Bontddu, by the entrance to Bontddu Hall, take a minor road angling away from the A496. Follow it up the valley to a small parking area just before the road crosses over the river (Pont Hirgwm) by a telephone box, or continue up the road to a parking area at its end.

Until the building of Turnpike roads in the late 18th and early 19thC, enabling good access along the Mawddach estuary and the coast, travelling and moving goods by pack horse between Harlech and Dolgellau, linking with other roads to London, required following ancient highways, possibly prehistoric in origin, across the mountains. Drovers also used these routes to move cattle from the coast near Harlech on their way to markets in England. Rising from Bontddu an important ancient road divides into two branches. One went to Harlech via Bwlch y Rhiwgyr and Tal-y-bont. The other took a shorter more direct route, but over a higher pass, to reach Harlech via Llanbedr, and may have been a summer route. It is also speculated that this well constructed route is a Roman road. During the 18thC, when local gentry were becoming increasingly anglicised, the old road was an important link via Dolgellau to London Society. Inhabitants of Bontddu would also walk part of this way on their arduous 5 mile walk via Bwlch y Llan to the 13thC parish church in Llanaber. Improvements to the old road were made in 1765 at the request of William Vaughan of

Cors y Gedol. In the 18th and early 19thC peat cut upon the mountain top was brought down the old road in trucks on sleds.

1 Cross the bridge and follow the attractive narrow road up to its end at the alternative start. Take a signposted bridleway through a small iron gate on the right. The bridleway guided by small white-capped posts rises to an inscribed milestone, marking the two branches of the old road. Go up the LEFT fork – Tal-y-bont – to a ladder-stile/gate. Follow the green track down to a gate and on past a ruin – *with Llawlech ahead. On nearby Bryn Castell is an ancient hillfort, and a medieval settlement.* After a ladder-stile the old road, now little more than a path, continues to cross the Afon Dwynant. After a gate, it becomes a walled track and passes the ruin of Rhos caerau – *a former staging post that once provided refreshments for passing travellers.* It then continues along the edge of a plantation, and passes through a gate. At the plantation corner go through another gate and across a stream, then past a green track on the left. After another stream, at a white topped post, where the track bends half-left towards a gate, keep straight ahead alongside a stream to cross a stone stile in the wall onto a green cross track beyond. *The old route to Llanaber church continued further along the valley.*

2 Here you have a choice. (For **Walk B** follow the track RIGHT, through a gate and on towards a ruin. After crossing a second stream, head half-LEFT up the gorse covered hillside to cross a visible ladder-stile at a wall junction. Continue ahead up the hillside and on past old workings. Now contour across the steep slope then descend to a wall corner. Follow the wall up to cross a ladder-stile. Head half-LEFT up the steep tussocky slope, over a wall, and on up to cross a ladder-stile bridleway descends between walls to a small gate, then continues down to reach your outward route at the inscribed milestone.

WALK 12

AROUND LLAWLECH

DESCRIPTION An exhilarating 8½ mile walk for experienced walkers, with panoramic views, following ancient highways over two high mountain passes, and an old drovers route along Cwm Ysgethin, to complete an upland circuit around Llawlech. Allow about 5 hours.
START Road end, Banc-y-Fran [SH 657202]
DIRECTIONS See **Walk 11**. Follow the minor road up to a parking area at its end.

I Follow instructions from the second sentence in paragraph **1** of **Walk 11**.

at the top of the bwlch at point **3**.) For **Walk A** continue ahead to follow the delightful old green track up across the open slopes to go through a small iron gate at the top of Bwlch y Rhiwgyr. Turn RIGHT and follow the stiled path alongside the wall up to the summit cairn on Llawlech, and on across the broad level ridge to reach a small gate, and stone cairn at the top of another bwlch, where you are joined by Walk B.

3 Go through the gate and follow this superb high-level green highway across the head of the valley and down to cross a ladder-stile below where a wall blocks its progress. Follow the delightful green track over further ladder-stiles on a long steady descent along Braich – *enjoying views of Cadair Idris ahead*. Later, after passing an old iron ladder-stile, ignore the track bending left to a gateway, but continue ahead on the waymarked bridleway. After a bridle gate the

2 Continue ahead to follow the delightful old green road up across the open slopes to a small iron gate at the top of Bwlch y Rhiwgyr, where you join the Ardudwy Way for the next few miles . Follow the path down the narrow pass, through gates, then on alongside a boundary, later becoming a narrow green track and passing stone circles in an adjoining field. After two ladder-stiles the track descends to a track junction. Turn RIGHT with the Ardudwy Way. Now follow a gated track for 2½ miles up and across expansive Cwm Ysgethin past Llyn Erddyn, following instructions in paragraph **2** of **Walk 9**. At the old Harlech road above Pont Scethin, turn RIGHT. Follow the old road up past the Janet Haigh memorial to the top of the bwlch at the northern end of the Llawlech ridge. Now follow instructions in paragraph **3** of **Walk 11**.

WALK 13

CUTIA CHAPEL & PANORAMA WALK

DESCRIPTION A 6 mile (**A**) walk of great variety exploring a delightful expansive upland area and wooded valleys north-east of Barmouth, offering great views. The route follows a scenic upland road to its end, then continues on a mainly level section of an ancient upland route walked by worshippers from Bontddu to the 13thC parish church at Llanaber, reaching a height of 880 feet before descending to Cutiau, with its early 19thC chapel. It then follows a delightful old walled 17thC route across wooded slopes for a stunning finale at the famous Panorama viewpoint, popular since Victorian times. Allow about 3½ hours. A shorter 3½ mile walk (**B**) is included.
START Snowdonia National Park Panorama car park [SH 625166]
DIRECTIONS Leave Barmouth on the A496 towards Dolgellau. At the end of Porkington Terrace turn left up Panorama Road. Follow the road for ¾ mile to the car park.

On the wooded hillside just above the northern edge of the estuary, lies the hidden hamlet of Cutia, containing a former chapel, with an interesting history. It was built in 1806, when the Congregationalists began teaching their doctrine locally. One of its prime promoters was a Mr Evans, originally from Llangollen, who opened a school in Barmouth to teach basic education and the gospel. On Sundays, he preached in Barmouth, Cutia, and Dyffryn, a commitment which affected his health. In 1826, members of the three communities asked that he serve as their pastor. Their written request included the enticement of 'regarding your sustenance, we of Cutiau promise to collect £8 a year'. At the time the chapel contained 20 members. He was only 24 years old, when he was ordained here on 23rd May 1827. Later a new chapel was built in Barmouth, and he travelled throughout Wales, raising £300 towards its cost of £600. In 1844, the Rev. James Jones took over, cleared the rest of the debt, and offered a bilingual service to English non-conformist visitors.

I Continue along the road, keeping ahead at the junction (no through road). Shortly it begins to rise – *giving excellent views across to Cadair Idris, along the Mawddach estuary to the distant Arans, and later of the long ridge leading up to Dyffwys.* Continue along this upland road past cottages. After just over 1 mile you go through a gate by a stream. About 50 yards further, where the road bends left up to Sylfaen, you have a choice.(For **Walk B** go through a gate on your right and down a stony track to pass along the right hand side of a large stone barn. Go through a gate at its far end to enter a field. Now follow the wall on your right, past a gate, to go through the gate facing you just beyond. Follow a path down through a wood to reach a waymark post opposite a low stone stile. Turn right and resume text at point **4**.) For **Walk A** continue up the road.

2 After going through another gate, the road bends down to nearby Sylfaen farm. Here take the signposted path through double gates ahead and follow a stony track past a large barn and up to a gate. Continue with the stony track past a small quarry. After a gate, the level track becomes the old church route as it heads across the expansive upland pasture towards Diffwys ridge, It passes above the remains of Golodd – *said to be where drovers left their cattle* – then a ruined stone barn, and through a gate. When the track splits take the green LEFT fork. After 30 yards at a stream, where a green track rises left up the hillside *(the old mountain road via Bwlch y Rhiwgyr to Tal-y-bont)*, turn RIGHT to cross a stone stile in the nearby wall. Walk alongside the stream to rejoin the stony track.

3 After crossing a stream, turn RIGHT along a green track, soon passing a large stone enclosure on the left. After a gate the track follows the wall to a gateway and continues to a signposted cross path. Here go through the large iron gate ahead. Follow the green track alongside the edge of the forest

– *soon with views down to Barmouth bridge, and Fairbourne beyond* – to join a lane. Follow it down past a nearby ruin – *said to be an old drovers' inn* – then a cottage. Just beyond a signposted path on the left go through the gated entrance to Tyddyn Pandy on the right. Go along its access track, soon descending into a wooded valley, over the river, and up to Tyddyn Pandy. After passing the front of the house, turn RIGHT past its gable end, then just before a stone barn ahead turn LEFT up across the wooded slope to reach a facing wall. Follow it LEFT down to go through a small gap in the bottom wall corner. Follow the wall on your right across the top of the bracken covered field to cross a ladder-stile. Follow the path down through the forest to eventually cross a low stone stile in a wall corner. Join a waymarked path ahead.

4 Follow the path through an area of deciduous woodland, later descending to a third ladder-stile by a gate. Continue with the path across the more open woodland of Coed y Tyn Llidiart. Shortly at a cross path descend LEFT alongside a wall past a pylon then follow the path to a small gate to pass between a house and Cutia chapel – *now private- ly owned.* Walk along the narrow driveway and on down the narrow lane. It bends left past a small roadside ruin – *said to have been a shop.*

5 When the lane bends down sharp left, with a iron gate ahead, turn RIGHT to follow a delightful narrow walled track through Coed Glan-y-Mawddach. *It was part of the 17thC Dolgellau to Barmouth road, used by travellers before the building of the turnpike road, now the A496.* At a signposted path junction, go up the RIGHT fork alongside a wall. This delightful path rises steadily through the trees. *After a while you will see below the ruin of Bwlch-y-Goedleoedd, reputed to be an old inn. The great 14thC Welsh poet, Dafydd ap Gwilym apparently stayed here. It is said that after his plan to meet 12 local young* women *at different times was discovered, he gladly retreated to his locked room at the inn!* A little further, you reach an iron gate on the left giving access to the Panorama Walk. Complete the short circuit to enjoy the stunning views, then continue along the walled path to emerge from the wood. Follow the path to Panorama Road by the start.

WALK 14

CWM DWYNANT

DESCRIPTION A 6¼ mile (**A**) or 5½ mile (**B**) walk exploring the foothills and quiet upland valleys on the northern side of the Mawddach estuary, once searched for gold. Allow about 4 hours.

START Snowdonia National Park Farchynys car park [SH 662186]

DIRECTIONS The car park adjoins the A496 just west of Bontddu.

1 Cross the A496 and turn LEFT. After about 100 yards take a signposted bridleway angling up to a gate into the forest. The bridleway rises steadily across the tree and rhododendron covered slope, soon alongside a wall. At its corner keep ahead up the bridleway to eventually leave the forest by a small wooden gate. Keep ahead – *enjoying views along the estuary to the railway viaduct, and Fairbourne, and back to Cadair Idris* – soon bending north. *Below is Caerdeon church, built in 1862 in the style of an Italian hillside chapel for private use, and consecrated as a church in 1887.*

2 Just beyond a ladder-stile go through a facing wooden gate in a wall to enjoy a short section of walled bridleway. After crossing a stream, the bridleway rises ahead, then continues up alongside a wall and an old track to a lane. Go up the lane. After Bwlch-yr-ysgol the lane descends to a signposted cross-path by a large stone. Here turn LEFT along the forestry road, passing above a lakeside seat – *a great stopping place* – and soon alongside a narrow section of oak trees on your right. Near their end at a few conifers, look for a path on the right angling down through the trees. The path continues alongside a wall. Just beyond its corner, at a path junction, you have a choice. (For **Walk B** turn right and follow the path down through the conifers to cross a ladder-stile. At a facing wooden gate ahead turn left down the old walled path to a small gate. Continue down to pass between Goetre Uchaf and Trenafon cottages to cross a bridge over the Afon Dwynant to reach a lane at point **3**.)

For **Walk A** continue ahead on an indistinct path through bracken and conifers on a gradual descent through the forest edge to reach a green track by farm buildings. Follow it down to the farmhouse, then descend its access track to a lane. Follow it RIGHT along the attractive Cwm Dwynant for nearly 1/2 mile to pass a telephone box.

3 Continue up the lane. Shortly take the RIGHT fork and follow this delightful narrow lane past Cae-mur Hywel – *near which was a trial for gold in 1862*. After a gate by Capel Moriah, angle LEFT across a grassy area to join a waymarked path beside a wall. At Cae Gwian, turn LEFT up a track, and at a track junction, keep ahead. The track rises through the trees. Shortly, take the greener RIGHT fork. *Nearby was a small and unsuccessful 1850s gold mine.* Soon you leave the mixed woodland by a gate. Continue along the track. *The dome-shaped Bryn Castell ahead contains an ancient hillfort and a medieval settlement.* Cross over the river, and just past an outbuilding, opposite Bwthyn Bach, turn LEFT and follow a meandering green track. When it bends left towards a large stone barn, turn RIGHT down through a line of trees and on across a reedy field to the wall above a cottage. Here, turn LEFT and go through a gate in the corner. Go up the right-hand field edge to a waymarked gate by a house (Gwyliwch-y-ci). Go past its left hand end and up its narrow access track to a stile by a gate. Continue to a waymarked stile ahead, then bear RIGHT, and after a few yards LEFT up alongside a wall. After a few yards, turn LEFT and follow a path up through the edge of the wood to soon leave it by a stile. Follow the nearby access track to join a road. Go down the road – *enjoying views from Diffwys to Cadair Idris* – past the entrance to Cae Hir, and Cae Goronwy. *Ahead on Clogau mountain are waste tips and an incline – a legacy of its gold -mining history.*

4 About 150 yards below Tynlon Uchaf, when close above the river, take a signposted path through a recessed gate on the right. Just beyond bear LEFT to pass round the large barn to go through a small gate

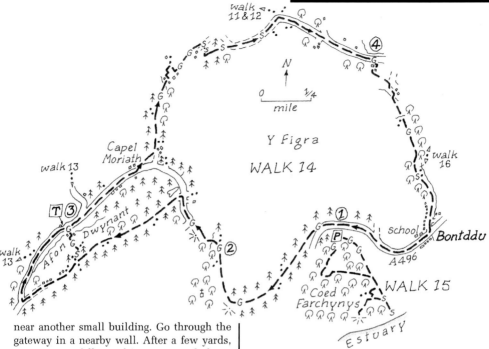

near another small building. Go through the gateway in a nearby wall. After a few yards, turn LEFT to follow a faint green track down a small ridge. At an access track, bear RIGHT to follow the waymarked path along a stony track past a barn. Just before a stream, turn LEFT above it to go through a waymarked wall gap ahead. Cross the stream to join a track. Shortly, as it rises half-right follow the waymarked path ahead down a field to a small gate in the left-hand corner. Follow the path above the narrow wooded valley, soon passing through gorse and bracken, to go between two old brick supports. Descend the incline and at a fence at the bottom bear RIGHT down a path to a ladder-stile to reach a track near the site of Figra Mill (See **Walk 16**). Continue ahead along the track past Hirgwn gorge, then down a road past houses to the A496 at Bontddu. Follow the road out of the village back to the start.

WALK 15
COED FARCHYNYS

DESCRIPTION A 1¼ mile undulating walk exploring an attractive predominantly oak woodland with viewpoints, owned by Snowdonia

National Park Authority, and including a visit to the edge of the Mawddach estuary. Allow about 1¼ hours.
START As **Walk 11**

Head across the grassy picnic area to a wooden kissing gate into Coed Farchynys. Follow the path up through the wood, shortly descending then later bending left and rising again in stages. After diverting to a nearby bench seat for a glimpse across the estuary, the path zig-zags down to a fence, then gradually descends to a track at the wood edge. Follow it RIGHT to a ladder-stile. Continue to another ladder-stile ahead at the estuary edge. Return to cross the first ladder-stile back into the wood. Now follow the track back to the start. Alternatively, for the more energetic, follow a path up through the trees to a fence and nearby viewing area. Return down the path. Later when it bends right take a path on the left across the slope and down to a waymarked path junction. Follow the path RIGHT down to rejoin the track. Follow it back to the car park.

WALK 16

CLOGAU

DESCRIPTION A fascinating 3 mile walk (**A**) tracing some of the area's gold mining history. The route takes you up the impressive wooded Hirgwm gorge, past the site of Figra Mill and the entrance to Clogau gold mine up to Pont Hirgwm. It then visits an important mine adit before rising across the upland pasture of Clogau mountain to a higher level mine at just over 800 feet. It descends a delightful green tramway then lane, before finishing by the Hirgwm gorge. Allow about 2 hours. The route can easily be shortened to a 1½ mile walk (**B**).
START Old bridge over Afon Hirgwm, Bontddu [SH 669187]
DIRECTIONS Leave Barmouth on the A496 towards Dolgellau to reach Bontddu. After passing the school and a garage take a minor road on the left. Immediately turn right over the river and park tidily. Alternative roadside parking is available further along the A496 on the right.

The steep-sided Hirgwm Valley and surrounding hills once echoed to the sound of mining, becoming one of the most important gold-mining areas in Britain. Small-scale mining, primarily for copper and lead, probably occurred here since before the Romans. Between 1825-45, Figra and Old Clogau mines, on opposite sides of the valley, were worked for copper. But a chance discovery of gold, worth thousand of pounds, on a spoil tip in 1854 led to the first of several gold rushes. The working of the gold bearing quartz veins, primarily the St. David's Lode, during the rest of the century, in what became known as the Clogau Mine, was undertaken by a series of companies, some shortlived. A gold rush in 1862 saw the existing company awarded a medal at the Great Exhibition. From 1898 to the early 1900s, mining was larger in scale, involving up to 63 men working above ground and 190 below, and producing a peak yield of 18,417 oz of gold in 1904. Mining has continued intermittently since then, producing the famous Clogau gold used to make wedding rings for the Royal Family. Most gold extraction involved adit mining – inclined tunnels driven by

hand until the 1870s when compressed-air drills were introduced. They provided access to the ore, drainage and ventilation.

Figra Mill, powered by a waterwheel, was built as a crushing mill to serve the copper mines, then adapted for gold production in 1862. A zig-zag track and incline connected the mill with Figra mine above. There were constant changes in machinery to improve the extraction of gold from pulverised quartz and reduce the gold being lost in the process. Mechanical crushing was done by 'stamps', heavy columns of wood and iron, requiring massive foundations and reinforcement of the river bank. At the end of the 19thC a new mill powered by a turbine was built, with a gas engine as standby. Just downstream was a smaller mill in use until the 1930s, whose Britten pans used mercury to extract the fine gold particles. In the 1890s high grade ore was brought here in locked boxes by Robin the donkey!

I After crossing the old bridge over the river Hirgwm go up the no through road past toilets and houses, then continue up a stony track above the impressive deep narrow wooded river gorge to level out at the remains of Figra mill. Cross nearby Figra Bridge over the river. Bear left up the stony path past a gated track leading to nearby houses (your return route). Follow the stony track ahead up the eastern side of the wooded valley, shortly levelling out to pass the secured entrance to Clogau mine – first worked in 1862, and connected by Llechfraith adit to the main workings on Clogau mountain in 1903. After a kissing gate/gate continue up a path through a more open area, briefly above the river, to a kissing gate onto a minor road near Pont Hirgwm. (For **Walk B** turn right to point **4**.)

2 Take the signposted path through the large gate opposite, and walk along the track, soon rising. After passing through a gap in the wall just before a hidden farm angle RIGHT up the slope to go through a gateway in the wall ahead, then turn LEFT alongside the wall down to cross a stile. Descend the slope to join a track at the end

of a long stone barn. Follow it RIGHT passing above a ruin, and by a waste tip to reach the gated entrance to the Ty'n-y-cornel adit. *Started in 1880 and reaching 1,102 feet by the end of 1881, then extended by a new company between 1888-90, it cost considerable effort and money, but for little return. Businessmen from Barmouth then profited from this hugh capital investment, employing about 25 men between 1891-98. Under a new company, between 1898-1903, as the workings were being extended, and the Llechfraith adit being dug, ore was transported from the adit mouth in 6 cwt buckets on a 1,100 yards aerial ropeway dropping 210 feet down to Figra Mill.* Return along the track and just before the gate by the barn do a sharp U-turn RIGHT then follow the wall on your left to cross a stile in the corner. Follow the wall on your left up the field, soon levelling out.

3 When joined by a wall on your right with a path continuing ahead, do a sharp U-turn RIGHT up beneath the wall to join a path, soon bending LEFT to a waymarker post at the wall corner. Follow the path beneath the wall, then at a small ruin in the wall – *with a good view of Diffwys* – go half-RIGHT to follow the path up the predominantly gorse covered hillside to a small gate in a wall. Continue up the path. When it levels out take another path to cross a nearby ladder-stile. *Nearby is a tip and drainage adit for one of two new mines worked in the late 1850s/early 1860s. On top of the mountain is the Old Clogau copper and gold mine. By 1865, a system of tramways and inclines were being built around the mountain to transport ore down to Figra Mill.* Turn RIGHT and follow the old tramway through two gates. Keep on with this delightful level green tramway. At a waymark post, when the tramway splits, go down the long RIGHT fork – *enjoying views to the estuary* – to a kissing gate. Continue with the old tramway down the hillside, passing through a gate. When it levels out,

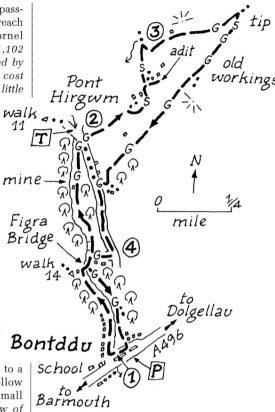

just before a gate and nearby cottage, bend sharp RIGHT down an enclosed onto a road. Follow the road LEFT down the valley.

4 Later take a signposted path down a driveway on the right past Vigra, then a track past another house to a gate to join your outward route beyond. Turn LEFT down the path. Just before Figra bridge, follow an enclosed path ahead to a kissing gate. Follow the path through the wood, soon descending to another kissing gate. Just below, take the lower path above Hirgwm gorge and on through the trees. Go through a small gateway and follow the enclosed path down the side of a house and a former chapel to the road near the start.

CWM GWYNANT & LLYNNAU CREGENNAN

DESCRIPTION This varied highly scenic 8 mile walk takes you through a stunningly beautiful area on the southern side of the Mawddach estuary, offering superb views. The route follows nearly 3 miles of the Mawddach Trail on the former Ruabon railway line along the estuary's wooded edge, before heading inland up the attractive wooded Cwm Gwynant. It then passes along a wide upland valley below the Cadair Idris range to the delightful Cregennan lakes, before descending in stages to Arthog. Allow about 5 hours.

START Lay-by beneath Arthog village hall [SH 637141] or Snowdonia National Park Arthog car park [SH 640148]

DIRECTIONS The lay-by lies on the A493 at the western end of Arthog. For the SNP car park proceed further east through the village, and just past Arthog Terrace, built in the 1860s, turn left by a green corrugated building along a minor road

It is hard to believe that to-day's tranquil estuary was once a hive of activity. Its creeks supported numerous shipyards attracted by the plentiful local oak, and between 1750 – 1865 some 318 vessels were launched on the Mawddach. There was also a flourishing trade in imported goods such as lime, coal, sugar, soap and candles, and in the export of woollen 'webs' , a coarse white cloth woven locally, and later, timber and slate. From 1869 steam trains ran regulary along the estuary on the Ruabon-Barmouth railway bringing many visitors into the area. As late as the 1950s, on Saturdays in summer, trains from different parts of England, full of passengers, many bound for Butlins in Pwllheli, passed this way. The line closed in 1965.

I Cross the road, and turn RIGHT along the grass verge. Shortly, take a signposted gated bridleway on the left to join the Mawddach Trail. Follow it RIGHT to pass the SNP car park on the site of the former Arthog Station. The Trail crosses a minor road and an iron bridge, then continues alongside the estuary. *Its saltmarsh is an important wildlife site for waders. The demand for housing slate led to several quarries being opened in the area. The visible Ty'n y Coed quarry operated between 1860 and the early 1880s, when high costs forced its closure.* After passing concrete Second World War 'tank traps' the Trail continues to an information board at the former Garth Siding, where once stood two cottages for railwaymen. *Finished slate travelled from the cutting shed in trucks down an incline and along a tramway, to be taken away by sailing boat from a nearby jetty. Later it was taken from here by train.* Continue ahead, past the remains of the old jetty and tramway. After a while, the estuary narrows – *where the clash between an incoming tide and the river is often more evident* – then widens again. Eventually you reach an information board at Abergwynant.

2 After crossing the bridge over the Afon Gwynant, turn sharp RIGHT down a stony track past a gate, then follow the track near the river along the edge of Abergwynant Wood. Shortly the track bears RIGHT through a gate. After another gate keep ahead up the lane to reach the A493. Cross the road, turn LEFT, then go up a side road. Follow this quiet road up the attractive wooded Gwynant valley close by the river for 1 mile to reach King's Youth hostel. Continue up the road and on the bend, follow the signposted path through a small gate and up through the wood to rejoin the road by a small ruined chapel and neat graveyard, still used today. Continue along the road and when it bends over the river, keep ahead along a green track to enter open country. Continue on the track towards a large stone house – *with good views south east to Cadair Idris.* When it fades, keep ahead to follow a waymarked path through an old gateway. Go up a field, through another gateway, and on up to a ladder-stile/ gate by a stream.

3 Continue up the path, which soon heads west along the wide upland valley by the

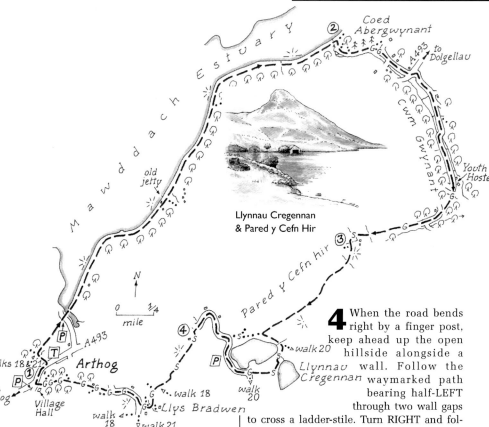

Coed Abergwynant

to Dolgellau

Mawddach Estuary

old jetty

N

0   ¼   mile

A493

P   T   Arthog

alks 18&21

to riog

Village Hall

walk 18   walk 21

Llynnau Cregennan & Pared y Cefn Hir

Cwm Gwynant

Youth Hostel

Pared y Cefn hir

walk 20

Llynnau Cregennan

walk 18   walk 20

Llys Bradwen

4 When the road bends right by a finger post, keep ahead up the open hillside alongside a wall. Follow the waymarked path bearing half-LEFT through two wall gaps to cross a ladder-stile. Turn RIGHT and follow the waymarked path across the hillside, through another wall gap and on over a ladder-stile. Go across the field to enter a walled track. Turn LEFT, and just beyond its end, turn RIGHT and walk along the field edge past a ruin to a gate ahead. Descend the stony track, past a side track and through another gate. Soon take a path angling down from the track to cross a delightful old stone clapper bridge. *Nearby upstream is the site of Llys Bradwen, reputed to have been the court of Bradwen, leader of one of the 15 tribes of North Wales in the early 12thC.* Turn RIGHT along a green track up to a road. Follow it down past Cregennan Farm. On the bend take the signposted bridleway through a gate marked Tyn-y-grai. Follow the stony track to another gate and on past Merddyn cottage. Follow the gated bridleway on a steady descent to reach a lane beneath Arthog village hall. Follow it down to the

nearby Cadair Idris range, passing beneath craggy Pared y Cefn hir – *on which is a Romano British hillfort.* After a while the larger of the Cregennan lakes appears ahead. As you near the lake, at a waymarker post, turn LEFT along the National Trust path, soon reaching the end of the lake. At the waymarked path junction cross the nearby footbridge and continue by the lake edge to cross two stiles. Turn LEFT and follow the waymarked path to the second lake then along its edge to cross a ladder-stile by a boathouse. Turn RIGHT and follow the path up by the wall and on to reach a road. Turn RIGHT and follow it by the lake, past a car park and toilets – *soon with stunning views down to Barmouth bridge.* Follow the highly scenic road meandering down the hillside, past a ruined cottage then Cefn-hir-isaf.

WALK 18

ARTHOG FALLS & LLYNNAU CREGENNAN

DESCRIPTION A 6½ mile (**A**) or 4½ mile (**B**) walk exploring the varied beautiful lowland and upland scenery around Arthog, offering stunning views. The route visits Arthog Bog, an SSSI then follows the Afon Arthog up a narrow wooded gorge past waterfalls to a clapper bridge near the medieval site of Llys Bradwen. Walk A extends on an upland circuit to visit one of the beautiful Cregennan lakes, owned by the National Trust. The joint route then crosses upland pasture, before descending through attractive woodland to a RSPB Nature Reserve, and on along a short section of the Mawddach Trail. Allow about 4½ hours for the full route.
START Lay-by beneath Arthog Village Hall [SH 637141] or Snowdonia National Park Arthog car park [SH 640148]
DIRECTIONS See **Walk 17**.

1 From the lay-by cross the road and turn RIGHT along the grass verge. Shortly, take a signposted bridleway on the left. Follow it through two gates to reach the Mawddach Trail. Go through the gate ahead, then follow the bridleway across Arthog Bog. *Known locally as Y Fawnog it contains many uncommon grasses and plants, attracting birds and butterflies. In the 19thC peat was dug up and taken away in sailing boats to be used as fuel.* When you reach two gates overlooking the estuary – *with views across to Barmouth* – go through the one on the right. Follow the signposted path, very briefly along a track, then round the edge of Arthog Bog to a small gate below an access lane and through small trees to a road. Follow it RIGHT over the Mawddach Trail, by the SNP car park on the site of the former Arthog Station.

2 Continue along the road by a small inlet – *with the castellated 17thC Arthog Hall prominent on the wooded hillside.* Shortly cross a ladder-stile on the left and follow the path, soon alongside the Afon Arthog, to reach the A493. Cross the road and turn LEFT, then take a signposted path through a small gate opposite St Catherine's Church. The path rises steadily up the wooded side valley above the river. After passing old stone gateposts go along the wide path ahead, then take a narrower waymarked path on the right. It rises through the trees, soon alongside the river cascading down a narrow rocky gorge. Just before small falls, the path bends away from the river and meanders up the wooded slope, then continues to a ladder-stile. The stiled path now rises past further falls to eventually reach a ladder-stile at the top below a cottage to join a green track just beyond. (For **Walk B**, follow instructions from paragraph 4.) Turn LEFT to cross a delightful nearby stone clapper bridge. Follow the path to join a track. *Nearby to your right is the site of two adjoining medieval buildings, known as Llys Bradwen, reputed to have been the court of Bradwen, leader of one of the 15 tribes of North Wales in the early 12thC.* Follow the track to a gate, and on past a side track up to another gate.

3 Continue ahead on the waymarked path along the field edge, past a ruin, then turn LEFT between walls to go through a waymarked gap in the wall on your right. Go across the field to a ladder-stile, then follow the waymarked path across the open slopes – *enjoying views across the estuary to Barmouth, the southern Rhinogs and the Lleyn peninsular* – through a wall gap, and on to a ladder-stile/gate just beyond a ruin. Go half-RIGHT to follow the waymarked path down through two wall gaps, then the field edge to join the road below. It rises steadily up the attractive hillside to suddenly arrive at the stunning sight of the larger of the Cregennan lakes – *part of an estate, gifted to the Trust in 1959.* Follow the road past a National Trust car park and toilets. Shortly, take a signposted path on the right across open ground to a stone stile. Keep ahead alongside the wall, then follow the path angling away onto a small rise. Go down the path and through a gate by a finger post. Continue down to another fingerpost, then bear RIGHT to follow the wall on your

5 At a waymarker post in a section of wall ahead, turn RIGHT alongside the boundary. After a ladder-stile/gate, turn LEFT alongside the wall down to its waymarked end. Turn LEFT and follow the waymarked path down the slope, then the edge of bracken – *enjoying good views towards Barmouth* – to a stile/gate. Continue with the path down through attractive woodland – *full of*

Estuary

Arthog Bog

Mawddach Trail

walk 17

to Dolgellau

falls

A493

Arthog

walks 19 & 20 Llynnau Cregennan

N

P

0   ¼
mile

walk 17

walk 20

Village Hall

walk 21

PB Reserve

to Fairbourne

Llys Bradwen

walk 21

left through three fields – *passing a small group of prehistoric stones in an adjoining field* – to join your outward route back over the clapper bridge.

4 Turn RIGHT up the green track, then LEFT along a road. Shortly, cross a stile on your right and go up the field to a ladder-stile ahead. Continue up alongside the wall to another ladder-stile in the corner – *with new views to Fairbourne and the coast.* Go down the field, over a ladder-stile, then half-LEFT across the slope and down to a waymarked fence corner by a house. Here angle back to a gate by the house, and continue along its access track. When it bends left by a roofless old stone barn keep ahead on a waymarked path beside the fence to cross a stile in it. Continue beside the fence to a ladder-stile. Keep ahead along the field edge, and at a stile on the left before a stream, turn RIGHT.

Clapper bridge

bluebells in Spring – to a stile at the bottom, then follow the nearby house's driveway down to the A493. Go along the road, then through a kissing gate on the left to enter Arthog Bog RSPB Nature Reserve. At the path junction ahead turn RIGHT and follow the path to a kissing gate and footbridge to join the tree-lined Mawddach Trail just beyond. Follow it RIGHT to join your outward route back to the start.

WALK 19

PARED Y CEFN HIR

DESCRIPTION A 4 mile walk exploring Open Access land adjoining Cregennan lakes. The route climbs up onto and along the exposed volcanic rocky ridge of Pared y Cefn hir (1247 feet) offering extensive views and the remains of an Iron Age hillfort. After descending its eastern end the route visits the nearby heather covered Pen Moelyn and its hidden attractive lake. It then returns along the valley beneath Pared y Cefn hir. This short but demanding walk with some scrambling, is for experienced walkers only and should be avoided in poor visibility. Allow about 2½ hours. It can easily be extended to incorporate Walk 20.

START National Trust Cregennan Lakes car park [SH 658143]

DIRECTIONS From Eldon Square in the centre of Dolgellau take the road heading west (Tywyn) out of town. After ¼ mile angle left along Cadair Road. Follow this minor road for 5 miles up into open country to the car park with toilets. The lakes can be also be reached from a shorter steep winding road signposted from the eastern end of Arthog on the A493.

1 Turn LEFT along the road past the lake up to a good viewpoint looking down to Barmouth bridge. Take the signposted path on the right to a ladder-stile, then the path's left fork up towards the prominent western rocky end of Pared y Cefn hir. At steeper rock take a path to the left of a narrow gully to eventually reach the top of the ridge – *offering all-round views*. Follow the path along the rocky heather ridge, overlooking an upland valley with Llyn Pen Moelyn visible ahead. *On this ridge are the remains of a Romano British hillfort*. The path then descends to a bwlch, before rising again to a small cairn at its highest point. The path now begins a steady descent from the ridge – *with old workings visible in the valley below* – to a post. Keep ahead to cross a stream to reach the bottom of a scree slope. Follow a path LEFT up the side valley.

2 After about 70 yards turn RIGHT up another path. It rises up the heather slope between ridges, then angles left to cross the ridge just below the flat heather summit of Pen Moelyn overlooking Llyn Pen Moelyn. Follow a path past the end of the reed and lilly covered lake and round its north western side to pass beneath a rocky ridge. At its end by a small pool continue along the path for about 20 yards, then head LEFT across the tussocky ground to reach the base of the heather/bilberry covered slope ahead. Turn RIGHT down an improving path towards a stone sheepfold, soon bending down the bottom edge of the heather slope to join your outward route at point **2**. Follow the path past the scree slope then along the bottom of the heather slope. It soon moves away and descends past a small post towards a large house below, passing to the left of a small gully to reach a wide cross path. Follow it RIGHT, soon heading south west along the wide upland valley beneath Pared y Cefn hir. *On its slopes are the remains of a cairn and a hut circle*. Later pass a waymarked NT path (Walk 20) and continue ahead to pass above the large lake to join your outward route at the ladder-stile.

WALK 20

CREGENNAN LAKES

DESCRIPTION A 3½ mile walk (**A**) around the Cregennan upland estate owned by the National Trust, featuring two beautiful lakes, the attractive valley beneath the imposing mountain of Tyrrau Mawr, and a standing stone. The route follows waymarked National Trust paths and attractive minor roads, including a section of Ffordd Ddu, an ancient mountain route (See Walk 25). Allow about 2½ hours. Shorter alternative 1¾ mile (**B**) and 1¼ mile (**C**) walks are included.

START National Trust Cregennan Lakes car park [SH 658143]

Cregennan Estate was gifted to the National Trust in 1959. On its upland plateau are two natural lakes, which are

Llyn Pen Moelyn

stocked with trout and managed as a fishery. The area contains standing stones, cairns and ancient trackways, evidence of prehistoric man's presence on this upland landscape.

I Turn LEFT along the road past the lake up to a good viewpoint looking down to Barmouth bridge. Take the signposted path on the right to a ladder-stile, then the lower path to pass above the large lake. Shortly, turn RIGHT to follow a National Trust waymarked path across open ground to a waymarked path junction at the end of the lake. (For **Walk B/C** cross the nearby footbridge and continue beside the lake edge to a ladder-stile/stream/step stile. Follow the waymarked path left to reach the smaller second lake. Continue along its edge to cross a ladder-stile by a boathouse. For **Walk C** turn RIGHT and follow the waymarked path up by the wall to the road. For **Walk B** follow the path ahead

alongside the lake then up to the road, which you follow past a nearby standing stone back to the start.)

2 For **Walk A** turn LEFT, over the stream and on to a ladder-stile. Turn LEFT and follow the waymarked path across upland pasture. Cross an old stony track, then follow the path round the right side of high ground ahead and up to a ladder-stile/gate at a good viewpoint into the valley dominated by the steep slopes and crags of Tyrrau Mawr. Follow the track down to a ladder-stile/gate by Nant-y-gwyrddail farm. Go past outbuildings then down the farm's access track to the valley road. Turn RIGHT along the road (Ffordd Ddu) – later rising to a cattle-grid and levelling out. At the junction turn RIGHT up the road. Just beyond a gate you have a choice. Either continue along the road past a nearby standing stone, or follow a National Trust path RIGHT down towards the lake then along its edge. At a ladder-stile by a boat house, turn LEFT to follow the waymarked path up to rejoin the road.

WALK 21

BENEATH CRAIG CWM-LLWYD

DESCRIPTION A 5½ mile walk exploring the attractive foothills lying south of Morfa Mawddach, offering panoramic views. Initially, the route follows the Mawddach Trail before rising steadily up through the hills above Arthog to join a short section of the scenic high-level Ffordd Ddu ancient trackway (See Walk 25) beneath the rocky escarpment of Craig Cwm-llwyd, reaching a height of over 1100 feet, before descending to pass 18thC Cyfanned Fawr and a nearby 19thC silver-lead mine. Allow about 4 hours. An equally enjoyable alternative to the Ffordd Ddu section is to follow the lower ancient upland road as shown.
START Morfa Mawddach Halt [SH 628141]
DIRECTIONS About 1 mile east of Friog, at a war memorial, take a side road off the A493 signposted to the railway halt at Morfa Mawddach, where there is a car park and toilets.

Morfa Mawddach, known as Barmouth junction until 1960, was once one of the busiest junctions in mid-Wales, offering through services to London, the Midlands and the North. It had 4 main platforms and was triangular to enable trains to change line without a turntable. Occasionally at night, passengers would alight here instead of Barmouth by mistake – did this confusion contribute to the name change? Often the sound of Welsh singing would be heard, so popular did its two refreshment rooms become with local people! The Mawddach Trail uses the former railway line to Ruabon. Opened in 1865 it was very popular with holidaymakers, but was closed in 1965.

I Join the Mawddach Trail by the toilet block, and follow it through the trees, over a lane, and on through a metal gate. Continue along the tree-lined Trail, passing an RSPB Nature Reserve site. After a further 1/3 mile, at a clear cross path, turn RIGHT and follow the gated bridleway to the A493.

Turn RIGHT along the grass verge. Shortly, just before the lay-by, take the lane on the left angling up towards the Village Hall. On the bend take the signposted bridleway up to go through two small gates. The bridleway now rises steadily up the edge of woodland, through another small gate, and on more steeply up the wooded hillside. After passing a side path to Buarth, the gradient eases, and soon you pass Merddyn cottage. Follow its stone access track to a road. Go up the road past Cregennan farm. *Soon an old iron seat provides an opportunity to rest and enjoy the extensive views over the estuary to Barmouth, and the Lleyn peninsular beyond. Ahead lies the western ridge of Cadair Idris.* Continue up the road, past a green track to a T junction. (For the alternative lower route turn right and follow the minor road to point **3**.)

2 Go through the gate ahead and follow the superb walled green track rising steadily up the hillside to a gate to join Ffordd Ddu. Go up this stonier track and through another gate. The track continues across the wild upland slopes beneath Craig Cwm-llwyd, soon rising steadily – *with panoramic views across to Barmouth and the Lleyn peninsula. Shortly, take a signposted path angling away alongside a wall on your right – soon passing a plaque recording the Americans who were tragically killed on their way home on the 8th June 1945. After a stile follow the path – a link to a lower ancient highway – across the reedy upland pasture – enjoying extensive coastal and mountain views – to a ladder-stile/ gate by a stream, then continue down to a stile by the forest corner. Follow the path along the edge of the clearing – in which is an old hut circle settlement – then through the conifers down to a road – another ancient road.*

3 Go through the kissing gate just below and follow a track round past Cyfanned Fawr. *This imposing quality stone building, dating from 1748, was once a house of some importance. In the middle of the last century, it was occupied by Morus Jones, a well known poet and winner of many bardic chairs. After one successful local eistedd-*

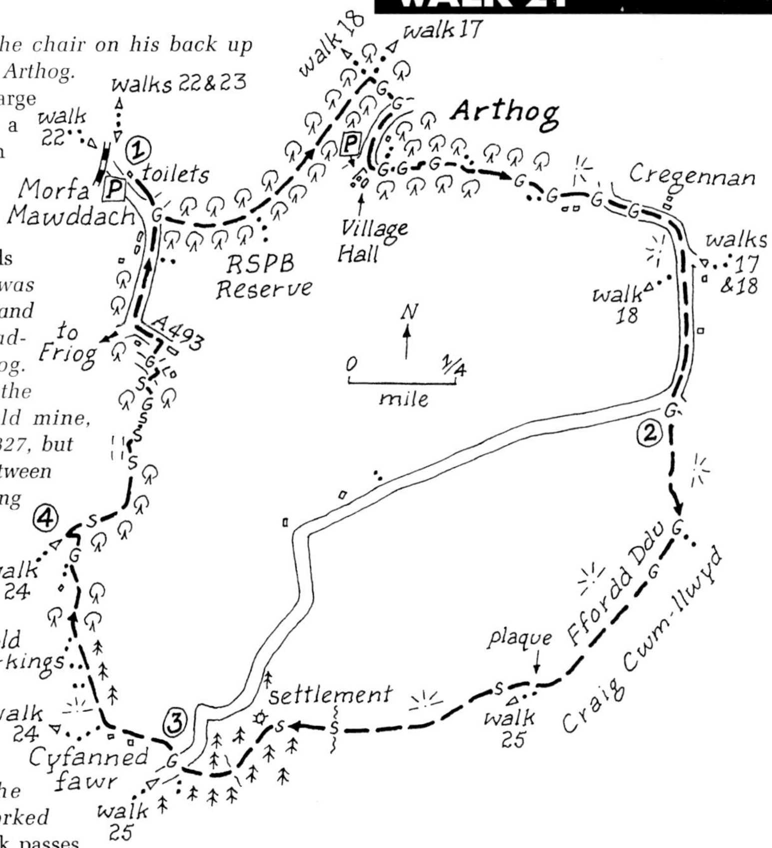

fod, he carried the chair on his back up the hillside from Arthog. After passing a large outbuilding, at a waymarked path junction, follow a delightful walled green track down the hillside towards Barmouth. *This was part of the old upland road network leading down to Friog. On your left are the remains of an old mine, first opened in 1827, but mainly worked between 1851-63, producing lead, copper and silver. Lead ore was taken to Penrhyn Point and by ferry to Barmouth from where it was shipped to Swansea for smelting and refining. In the 1880s it was worked for slate.* The track passes

[Map showing the walk route with labels: walk 18, walk 17, walks 22 & 23, walk 22, Arthog, Morfa Mawddach, toilets, Cregennan, P, Village Hall, RSPB Reserve, walks 17 & 18, walk 18, to Friog, A493, N, 0 — ¼ mile, old workings, walk 24, walk 24, settlement, plaque, Fforad Ddu, Craig Cwm-llwyd, walk 25, Cyfannedd fawr, walk 25, numbered points 1, 2, 3, 4]

along the bottom edge of a small wood and continues down to a gate/ kissing gate. The path then descends through birch to reach a waymarked path junction.

4 Here, do a sharp U-turn RIGHT and follow the path to a stile. Continue along the wooded valley. *Between the mid-1860s and 1873, slate was extracted from nearby Tyddyn Sieffre quarries, by companies which both went into liquidation.* After a ladder-stile by a small clearing follow the path through gorse, and at a gate on the adjoining track, turn RIGHT to follow the waymarked path alongside the wall, crossing two ladder-stiles. Keep ahead to a kissing gate, then descend steps and follow the path down through bracken, then trees past a small old quarry and on down to a lad-

der-stile. The path now descends to a track by Bryniau Mawddach. Follow it down to go through a kissing-gate at the nearby track junction, then descend the path to the A493 by Glasfryn Terrace. Cross the road and follow it LEFT – *past a garage bearing the old Arthog railway halt sign* – then at the war memorial turn RIGHT and follow the road back to the start. *Your return route follows the line of a 3 foot gauge tramway built in 1899, by the entrepreneur Solomon Andrews from Tyddyn Shieffrey tips to Morfa Mawddach, initially to carry quarry waste and materials for the building of houses. like Glasfryn and St Mary's Crescent, and roads. It was part of a network of tramways built to help realise his ambitious but unfulfilled plans for developing the area into a holiday resort (See **Walk 22**).*

WALK 22

BARMOUTH BRIDGE

DESCRIPTION A 3¾ mile walk, with superb views, over the magnificent 19thC rail and toll footbridge across the tidal mouth of the Mawddach estuary, following the Mawddach Trail on the former railway line to Ruabon, to visit Arthog Bog Nature Reserve. Allow about 2 hours.
START Harbour, Barmouth [SH 616154]

The railway viaduct stretching for ½ mile across the mouth of the estuary is one of the wonders of Wales. Built in 1867 it consists of 113 spans supported by over 500 timber piles. Its original 'drawbridge' over the navigation channel was replaced in 1899 by the current steel swing bridge, which requires eight men to operate manually. For a few months as the bridge was nearing completion, passengers were taken over the bridge in a carriage drawn by two horses. This must have been quite a sight! The railway gave local people access to various parts of Britain, and brought in many middle class Victorian visitors. Thankfully the bridge has survived closure threats, notably in 1980 from damage caused by the teredo worm.

I Follow the nearby main road out of Barmouth towards Dolgellau. At Porkington Terrace (1870), take the pathway opposite down past the Lifeboat Station to the bridge toll booth. Go across the bridge – enjoying the extensive views – then continue with the path alongside the railway. Near a small gate on the left, just before Morfa Mawddach halt once stood a refreshment and waiting room built in 1899 at the start of a horse-drawn tramway – still visible. Both were part of ambitious plans by Solomon Andrews, a remarkable self-made businessman, to develop the nearby area into a resort as he had at Pwllheli. The tramway took visitors to the estuary, then in 1903, on a circuit of Fegla Fawr, passing the three storey Mawddach Crescent he had built. After then his plans came to an end. Continue

past Morfa Mawddach halt and toilets on the Mawddach Trail and over a lane.

2 Go through a metal gate, and on along the tree-lined Trail, then take a waymarked RSPB path on the right to enter Arthog Bog Nature Reserve. Follow the path to a nearby gate and on to reach a cross-path. Follow it RIGHT to the road. Turn RIGHT and follow the road past St Mary's Crescent and back to Morfa Mawddach halt. Now make another enjoyable crossing over Barmouth bridge.

WALK 23

THE MOUTH OF THE MAWDDACH

DESCRIPTION An unusual 3½ mile walk that starts with a ferry crossing and features two living pieces of railway history and great views. The route takes the ferry across to Porth Penrhyn – the terminus of the Fairbourne and Barmouth narrow gauge steam railway – then heads towards Fairbourne, before taking an embanked path across the salt-marsh edges to Morfa Mawddach. It then returns by the historic railway/toll bridge across the estuary. Allow about 2½ hours. The walk can be combined with a railway trip into Fairbourne. The daily ferry operates from April to September and is subject to tide and weather.
START Harbour, Barmouth [SH 616154]

From earliest times a ferry has provided an important link between settlements. Once it was run by local monks from Ynys y Brawd, then a small island. After the Reformation it was run by local fishermen. In the 19thC, it was owned by the Barmouth Harbour Trust, and Penrhyn Farm on Porth Penrhyn played a key role in its operation. There were two boats, one for passengers, and the other for animals, wheeled vehicles, general goods and the Royal Mail. Inevitably, traffic greatly decreased with the arrival of the railway in 1867. In the 20thC, the ferrymen came to rely upon the Fairbourne narrow gauge railway for a living.

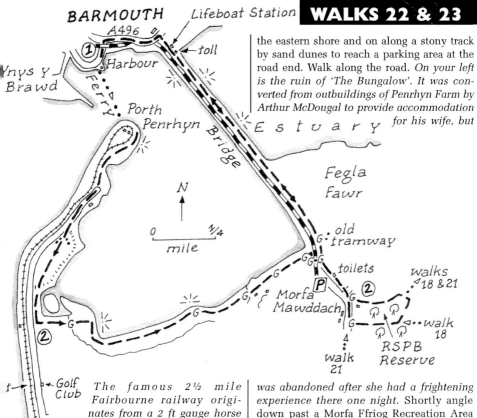

the eastern shore and on along a stony track by sand dunes to reach a parking area at the road end. Walk along the road. *On your left is the ruin of 'The Bungalow'. It was converted from outbuildings of Penrhyn Farm by Arthur McDougal to provide accommodation for his wife, but*

The famous 2½ mile Fairbourne railway originates from a 2 ft gauge horse drawn tramway built by Arthur McDougal (of flour fame) in 1895, initially for transporting materials for the building of Fairbourne, but extended to the ferry between 1897-98 and used to carry summer visitors. In 1916 the tramway was sold and converted into a miniature steam railway, which opened in 1919. Since then it has had a chequered history, experiencing many changes of ownership, periods of prosperity and decay, and severe flooding damage. But it has survived into the 21stC and continues to delight passengers to-day as the original tramway did in the late 1890s!

I Take the ferry over to Porth Penrhyn and make your way up the sand and shingle to the Barmouth Ferry Station and Harbour View cafe. Walk along the edge of

was abandoned after she had a frightening experience there one night. Shortly angle down past a Morfa Ffriog Recreation Area board then take the middle of three wide paths across open rough pasture, later passing another board at an embankment by a small tidal inlet and on to reach the road.

2 Here take a signposted path along the broad embankment overlooking the golf course – *built as part of McDougal's unfulfilled grandiose plan to develop Fairbourne into an elite resort. The grass-topped stone embankment, built in the 19thC as a sea defence, divides the extensive salt-marsh from land reclaimed to provide pasture for cattle and sheep, and later for the building of Fairbourne.* Follow the embanked path to eventually reach the mainline railway at Morfa Mawddach. Heed the warning signs before crossing the line, and go through a gate opposite. Turn LEFT and follow the path alongside the railway line and on over the railway/toll bridge, past the lifeboat station to reach the A496. Follow the road back into Barmouth.

WALK 24

ABOVE FRIOG

DESCRIPTION A 4 mile walk exploring the valleys and hills above Friog, with great views, and finishing with a fine stretch of coast. The route, which is accessible by train and bus, leaves Fairbourne to head up the Panteinion valley to follow an ancient route rising to about 750 feet, from where it descends past old slate quarries to Friog. The route then passes through the village and returns by Fairbourne Beach. Allow about 3 hours. By using the road through Friog, the route can easily be undertaken as two separate circuits : a Fairbourne walk of 2 miles and an inland walk of 2½ miles starting from Friog.
START Fairbourne Station [SH 614129]
DIRECTIONS Turn off the A493 into Fairbourne. After crossing the main railway line, turn right to a car park and toilets by shops.

Friog was originally a farming community that later developed through the working of two adjacent slate quarries on the southern side of the narrow Panteinion valley, opened by Dr. George Walker (1807-1884), a Nottinghamshire surgeon, renowned as a sanitary reformer. Interestingly, his gravestone in the Quaker burial ground at Bryn Tallwyn, Llwyngwil acknowledges his role in providing employment for many local people for nearly a quarter of a century. Henddol operated between 1865-71, and was later reworked in 1883. The Goleuwern quarry was opened in 1867, employing 51 men by 1872, the highest paid being the masons, then the blacksmiths, then labourers. Slate was brought down a long incline to the valley road, then taken by cart to the ferry. From the early 1890s, both quarries operated under one company, employing over 80 men. They finally closed in the late 1920s.
In the quarry, which is privately owned, is the 'blue lake', which featured in local tourist brochures. It is a 40 ft deep quarry pit that was deliberately filled with water in 1901 by Arthur McDougal's engineer to be used as a reservoir in a scheme for providing Fairbourne with electric lighting. Pipes were laid but the scheme progressed no further.

I Cross the railway line and follow the road out of Fairbourne to the A493. Turn RIGHT and just past the garage, turn LEFT up Ffordd yr Ysgol. After about 30 yards, go through a kissing gate up on the right and follow the path alongside the school fence up to another kissing gate. Continue up through trees to a small gate, then up the part-wooded slope – *with the quarries visible ahead* – soon bending RIGHT to a gate by a house. At its far corner turn LEFT to a small gate between outbuildings. Go across the access track and follow the waymarked path past a small stone barn. Just beyond the end of a modern barn, go through a waymarked gate. Follow the path through the trees then down to a road by the river. Follow it LEFT up the wooded valley past a narrow waterfall on the bend – *called 'Henddol Fall' in an 1863 guide.*

2 Just before Panteinion Farm, take a signposted path through a gate up on your right and follow it up to a kissing gate. Continue with the path keeping with its left fork by the fence along the edge of the valley. This delightful green path – *a branch of the higher ancient mountain road network* – then begins to rise. At a waymarked path junction go up the RIGHT fork, soon bending right up to a kissing gate/ gate. Continue ahead, taking the LEFT fork of a green track up the hillside. It climbs more steeply beneath a small plantation, then levels out to cross a stream. Go through a gateway and past a track leading down to old workings. *Between 1851-63 a mine here produced lead, copper and silver. In the 1880s it was worked for slate. Keep ahead up the now walled track.*

3 Just beyond its end, with the stone barn of 18thC Cyfanned Fawr (See Walk 21) ahead, turn RIGHT by a waymarker post set in the wall. Follow the wall on your right to go through an old gateway. Descend the path's waymarked right fork, through another old gateway to cross a stream. Follow the waymarked path down near the stream. At a ruined stone barn, turn LEFT along its near side, and at its corner, angle RIGHT through bracken to reach a waymarker post on a small ridge at a good viewpoint. Just below turn

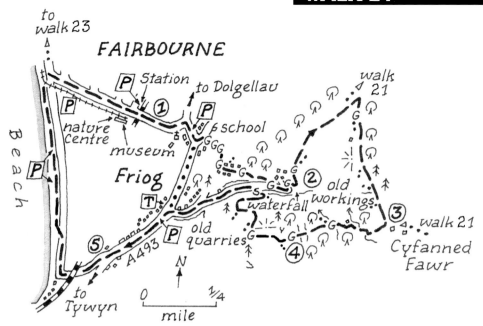

to walk 23

FAIRBOURNE

Station to Dolgellau

walk 21

nature centre

museum

s school

Friog

waterfall

old workings

old quarries

walk 21

Cyfanned Fawr

Beach

to Tywyn

N

0 ¼ mile

LEFT to follow the waymarked path down through trees to go through a kissing gate and across a stream just before it tumbles down a narrow gorge. Continue ahead on the main path through bracken, soon descending, then continuing through woodland.

4 Go through a kissing gate and follow the waymarked path up to a track. Follow it down to a kissing gate beneath quarry waste tips. Continue down the meandering stone track, past an impressive narrow entrance to the quarry, to reach a road in the wooded valley. Follow it to the A493. Cross the road and turn LEFT along the pavement through Friog.

5 By the old tollgate cottage, go along the minor road, soon passing through an arched railway bridge to reach the seafront. *Building the railway across the nearby steep cliffs was a major feat of engineering. Strangely, there were almost identical accidents on this section of line in 1883 and 1930, when the engine of the early morning train crashed onto the beach below, killing the engine driver and fireman. If the tide is out, walk back along the beach to Fairbourne. Otherwise, continue with the* road, then go along the grass embankment by the sea defences, through the beach car park, and on along a pathway. Shortly, turn RIGHT along Beach Road back to the start..

Fairbourne owns its existence to Arthur McDougal (of flour fame). In 1895, he purchased the Ynysfaig estate and adjacent land, with the intention to create an elite sea-side resort, to be called South Barmouth. His ambitious plans, which included a pier, were never fully realised by the time he sold the estate in 1912, being unable to compete with the better facilities of Barmouth. The village takes its name from the new railway station he had built in 1899 – a seemingly inappropriate English name in such a Welsh setting. Apparently, locals requested it be called 'Ynysfaig', but he refused on the grounds that the name boards had already been painted! The golf course and some original houses, at which he planted a rose bush, remain. Perhaps his greatest legacy was the horse drawn tramway, built originally for construction work, but extended to the ferry between 1897-98 and used to transport summer visitors. Without it the famous narrow gauge railway would never have developed.

CWM-LLWYD

DESCRIPTION An exhilarating 10 mile walk on superb scenic high-level ancient trackways across open hills and upland valleys, with panoramic views, and featuring many ancient sites and monuments. The route rises from Llwyngwril to follow a prehistoric route across foothills, passing standing stones and an early settlement. It then rises again to follow Ffordd Ddu across steep slopes, reaching a height of 1315 feet, before descending through Cwm-llwyd. Another ancient trackway is then followed before a descent by lane past Castel y Gaer hillfort. Allow about 6 hours.

START Llwyngwril [SH 592097]

DIRECTIONS Llwyngwril, with its own railway station, lies on the A493 coast road. On the northern side of the village centre is a signposted car park.

Ffordd Ddu (Black Road) is an ancient mountain route running from Dolgellau to Llanegryn, from where other routes led into the valleys of the Dysynni and Dovey, and on through the Upper Severn valley to the English border. It had branches down to Arthog, Friog and Llwyngwril. It is believed to be part of the Roman Road network linking West Wales with garrisons at Chester and near Shrewsbury, a route serving smaller camps near the coast. During the Middle Ages it became an important route for local Welsh gentry seeking patronage with London and the Royal Court. It also attracted bandits, especially the notorious 'Red Men of Dinas Mawddwy'. It was used regularly as a coach road until the building of the Turnpike coastal road in the 19thC.

I Follow the A493 north through the village towards Friog. After about ⅓ mile, take a signposted bridleway along a track on the right to its end by Llwyn Du. *An information board tells you about the house's connection with the Quakers.* Go through a gate ahead. Bear RIGHT then LEFT up the waymarked bridleway along the edge of a small wood – *associated with ancient Druid ceremonies* – to a gate. Follow the walled bridleway up the hillside, then go up a lane and through a gate. When it bends right towards a house, go up an enclosed green track ahead, soon bending up across the open gorse covered hillside – *offering panoramic coastal views* – to a gate. Continue with the track.

2 After another gate continue along the track – *enjoying stunning new views across to Barmouth* – soon heading inland to join a minor road. Follow the gated road – *known locally as Ffordd Sarnau* – soon rising steadily across upland country. *Just after sheepfolds, in the field on your left are five prehistoric standing stones, two having fallen. Further down the field are hut circles.* Continue along the road. *Later, on the slope below a fence on the left are the distinctive remains of a large Romano British hut circle settlement.* The road then descends, passing two further standing stones, then goes through a plantation. At a finger post on the right, take the second signposted wide path angling up through the forest, then along the edge of a clearing – *containing a hut circle settlement* – to a stile into upland pasture.

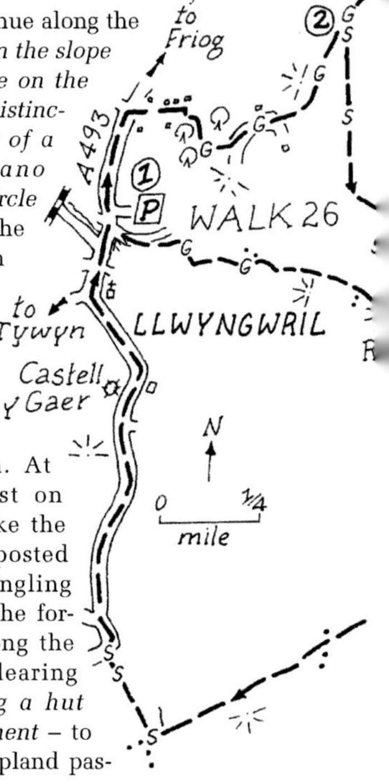

3 Follow the path up to a ladder-stile/ gate by a stream, and on across the reedy upland pasture to a stile. The path passes a commemorative plaque to a tragic plane crash to join a track above. *This is Ffordd Ddu.* Follow this superb high-level gated track rising steadily across the steep slopes of Braich Ddu and on past a plantation. It then

[Map showing: to Friog, A493, WALK 26, to Tywyn, Castell y Gaer, LLWYNGWRIL, N, 0 – ¼ mile]

begins a long gentle descent south through Cwm-llwyd, following the course of the Afon Dyffryn below, surrounded by bare hills. After crossing a stream, it heads south-west along the wide river valley.

plaque

walk 21

③

walk 21

standing stones

settlement

standing stones

sheepfolds

WALK 25

4 About 200 yards after a cattle grid beneath sheepfolds take another stony track angling RIGHT off Ffordd Ddu. Follow it across the flat reedy valley bottom, past old quarry workings by a tiny tree-lined gorge and waterfall. Later, after a gate by

Cwm-llwyd

Afon Dyffryn

sheepfolds

④

tips

iau

sheepfolds

sheepfolds, the stony track rises steadily to another gate. Continue along the track – *now with coastal views* – later passing a tiny plantation. At a track junction keep ahead following a line of telegraph poles – *with views of the Tarren Hills and Tywyn*. Later cross a ladder-stile in a wall corner just before a twin telegraph pole and gate. Go ahead through two fields to reach a road. Turn RIGHT along this attractive minor road, and at the junction bear RIGHT. Later the road descends past the remains of Castell y Gaer Iron Age hillfort to reach the main road at Llwyngwril. Follow the road through the village to the start.

WALK 26
RHIW-CORNIAU

DESCRIPTION A short but rewarding 2¾ mile walk exploring the upland area adjoining Llwyngwril featuring two ancient standing stones, a delightful walled bridleway and panoramic coastal views. Allow about 2 hours.
START Llwyngwril [SH 592097] See **Walk 25**.

1 Follow instructions in paragraph **1** of **Walk 25**.

2 Just before another gate cross a stile on the right and angle back across the field past two standing stones to a ladder-stile in the wall corner. Go across the next field. Shortly angle up the field to join the fence. At its top corner turn RIGHT then angle LEFT down to a ladder-stile/gate in the wall. Keep ahead to go through a gate on the right. Go down the field, cross the stream and follow the old embanked boundary down to a gate on a track above Rhiw-corniau. Follow the track (a bridleway) past the house overlooking Cwm Gwri and down over a cattle-grid. Continue down the track then at a gate, turn LEFT down the waymarked walled bridle-way to a gate. Continue down the bridleway. Later at a facing wall the bridleway bends RIGHT and descends to gates in the corner before a final short descent to a road at Llwyngwril. Follow it to the main road by the Garthanghared inn, which makes a good finish to the walk.

PRONUNCIATION

These basic points should help non-Welsh speakers

Welsh	English equivalent
c	always hard, as in **c**at
ch	as in the Scottish word lo**ch**
dd	as th in **th**en
f	as **f** in o**f**
ff	as **ff** in o**ff**
g	always hard as in **g**ot
ll	no real equivalent. It is like 'th' in **th**en, but with an 'L' sound added to it, giving **'thlan'** for the pronunciation of the Welsh 'Llan'.

In Welsh the accent usually falls on the last-but-one syllable of a word.

KEY TO THE MAPS

- ➞ Walk route and direction
- Metalled road
- Unsurfaced road
- •••• Footpath/route adjoining walk route
- River/stream
- Trees
- Railway
- **G** Gate
- **S** Stile
- **F.B.** Footbridge
- Viewpoint
- **P** Parking
- **T** Telephone
- Caravan site

About the author, David Berry

David is an experienced walker with a love of the countryside and an interest in local history. He is the author of a series of walks guidebooks covering North Wales, where he has lived and worked for many years, and has been a freelance writer for Walking Wales magazine. He has worked as a Rights of Way surveyor across North Wales and served as a member of Denbighshire Local Access Forum.

Whether on a riverside ramble, mountain or long distance walk, he greatly appreciates the beauty, culture and history of the landscape and hopes that his comprehensive guidebooks will encourage people to explore on foot its diverse scenery and rich heritage.

THE COUNTRY CODE

Be safe – plan ahead and follow relevant signs

Leave gates and property as you find them

Protect plants and animals, and take your litter home

Keep dogs under close control

Be considerate to other people

Open Access

Some routes cross areas of land where walkers have the legal right of access under The CRoW Act 2000 introduced in May 2005. Access can be subject to restrictions and closure for land management or safety reasons for up to 28 days a year. Details from: www.naturalresourceswales.gov.uk.
Please respect any notices.

Thanks to David of Benar Beach Camping Park, Tal-y-bont, for suggesting Walk 6.

Published by **Kittiwake-Books Limited**
3 Glantwymyn Village Workshops, Glantwymyn, Machynlleth, Montgomeryshire SY20 8LY
© Text & map research: David Berry 2010
© Maps: Kittiwake 2010
New edition 2010. Minor revisions 2013, 2017.
Cover photographs by David Berry – large: View from Barmouth towards Cadair Idris.
Inset: Pont Scethin (Walk 9).
Care has been taken to be accurate. However neither the author nor the publisher can accept responsibility for any errors which may appear, or their consequences. If you are in doubt about any access, check before you proceed.
Printed by Mixam, UK.
ISBN: 978 1 902302 81 2